First World War
and Army of Occupation
War Diary
France, Belgium and Germany

50 DIVISION
Divisional Troops
253 Brigade Royal Field Artillery
19 April 1915 - 16 November 1916

WO95/2820/1

The Naval & Military Press Ltd
www.nmarchive.com
Published in association with The National Archives

Published by

The Naval & Military Press Ltd

Unit 10 Ridgewood Industrial Park,

Uckfield, East Sussex,

TN22 5QE England

Tel: +44 (0) 1825 749494

www.naval-military-press.com

www.nmarchive.com

This diary has been reprinted in facsimile from the original. Any imperfections are inevitably reproduced and the quality may fall short of modern type and cartographic standards.

© Crown Copyright
Images reproduced by permission of The National Archives, London, England, 2015.

Contents

Document type	Place/Title	Date From	Date To
Heading	WO95/2820 50 Div 253 Bde RFA Apr 15-Nov 16		
Heading	50th Division 4th Northumbrian Bde Became 253rd Bde RFA Apr 1915-Nov 1916		
Heading	50th Division 4th Northbn Bde R.F.A. Vol I April		
War Diary	Newcastle	19/04/1915	19/04/1915
War Diary	Southampton	20/04/1915	20/04/1915
War Diary	Havre	21/04/1915	23/04/1915
War Diary	Boeschepe	24/04/1915	24/04/1915
War Diary	W of Abeele	25/04/1915	31/07/1915
Heading	50th Division 114th Northbn Bde RFA. Vol II From 1-31.8.15		
War Diary		01/08/1915	31/08/1915
Heading	1/2 Nbrn Bde RFA Am Col Vol XII		
Heading	50th Division 4th Northumbrian Bde R.F.A. Vol III Sept 15		
War Diary		01/09/1915	30/09/1915
Heading	50th Division 1/4th Northumbrian Howitzer Bde. Oct. 1915. Vol IV		
War Diary	Armentieres	01/10/1915	24/10/1915
War Diary	W. Hazebrouck	25/10/1915	31/10/1915
Heading	50th Division 1/4th Northumbrian Bde R.F.A. Nov Vol V		
War Diary	Hazebrouck	01/11/1915	01/11/1915
War Diary	M Cacetre	09/11/1915	30/11/1915
Heading	50 1/4th Northumbrian Bde (How) R.F.A. Dec Vol VI		
War Diary	Alar Caealac	01/12/1915	01/01/1916
Heading	50 1/4 North G 1 Bde R.F.A. Jan 1 Feb Vol VIII		
War Diary		01/01/1916	31/01/1916
Heading	50 1/4 Nbrn Bde RFA Vol IX		
War Diary		01/02/1916	31/03/1916
Heading	50 1/4 Nbrn Bde RFA Vol X		
War Diary		01/04/1916	31/08/1916
Heading	50th. Divisional Artillery 253rd. Brigade R.F.A. 50th. Divisional Artillery September 1916.		
War Diary		01/09/1916	16/11/1916

WO95/2820

50 Div.

253 Bde RFA

Apr '15 - Nov '16

50TH DIVISION

4TH NORTHUMBRIAN BDE
BECAME 253RD BDE RFA
APR 1915-NOV 1916

BDE BROKEN UP

121/6357

50th Division

4th both the Bde R.F.A.
Vol I
April — 31-4-15

Ap 15
Nov 16

19/4 — 1/6

Army Form C. 2118.

WAR DIARY
or
INTELLIGENCE SUMMARY.

4th North'n Bde
RFA

(Erase heading not required.)

Instructions regarding War Diaries and Intelligence Summaries are contained in F. S. Regs., Part II. and the Staff Manual respectively. Title pages will be prepared in manuscript.

Hour, Date, Place	Summary of Events and Information	Remarks and references to Appendices
April 19th - Newcastle	Brigade entrained left by three trains the last of which departed at 1-5 A.M. April 20th	
April 20th Southampton	Arrived SOUTHAMPTON and embarked on S.S. ANGLO CANADIAN and S.S. HURONIA	
3 A.M. April 21st HAVRE	Arrived HAVRE & commenced to disembark at 10 A.M. Entrained for an unknown destination at 10 P.M.	
1 A.M. April 22nd HAVRE	Left HAVRE at 1 A.M. arrived HAZEBROUCK at 8 P.M. arrived and marched to 4th Bty Ammn. Col. 1½ miles N. of BORRE - 5th Bty + Bde. H.d. Qrs. PRADELLES were in bivouacked	
2 P.M. April 23rd	Bde. arrived to proceed to BOESCHEPE. Arrived at midnight. Bivouacked.	
1 P.M. April 24th BOESCHEPE	Bde. orders to return to BORRE and PRADELLES arrived about 4-30 P.M. + on arrival received orders to proceed same night to a point about 1 mile W. of ABEELE. left at midnight running transport. Major T. A. Stagg motor cyclist to hospital with pneumonia	
9 A.M. April 25th W. of ABEELE	arrived 9 A.M. went into Billets.	
evening of April 26th "	Bde. orders to march to a point 1½ miles N.E. of STEENVOORDE. Marched via WATOU. arrived 9.45 P.M.	

Army Form C. 2118.

WAR DIARY
or
INTELLIGENCE SUMMARY.
(Erase heading not required.)

Instructions regarding War Diaries and Intelligence Summaries are contained in F.S. Regs., Part II. and the Staff Manual respectively. Title pages will be prepared in manuscript.

Hour, Date, Place	Summary of Events and Information	Remarks and references to Appendices
Afternoon 27th April.	Recd. orders to march to RYVELD. Arrived 6.30 P.M.	
28th-29th-30th April	Routine.	
1st + 2nd May.	Routine.	
Afternoon 3rd May.	Received orders to march to LE TEMPLE.	
4th + 5th May.	Routine.	
12.30 A.M. 6th May.	Recd. orders to march to a point 1000× W. of VLAMERTINGHE. Marched 1 A.M. + arrived at 6.30 A.M. O.C. Bde. + O.C. 4th & 5th Bdys. + Adjt. spent the morning making a reconnaissance for positions to be occupied by night. At 8.P.M. Batty. proceeded to occupy positions as follows. 4th Bdy. just N. of MENIN ROAD + 3000× E. of YPRES, 5th Batty. 300× S. of LA BRIQUE + 1000× N.E. of YPRES. Wagon lines were established 500× E. of VLAMERTINGHE on the POPERINGHE — YPRES ROAD. The Bde. Amm. Col. moves up to BRANDHOEK + Bde. Hd. Qrs. was fixed there also. Both batteries were attached to 28th Division. 4th Bdy. being Army Troops under O.C. 3rd Bde. R.H.A., 5th under O.C. 31st Bde. R.F.A.	
May 7th	Batteries in action — 4th Bdy. fired 20 rounds — 5th Bdy. fired 16 rounds.	
May 8th	Batteries in action — 4th Bdy. fired 392 rounds (had casualties: Killed By. Gregg. Wounded Sgt. Watson. Br. Thorne.) 5th Bdy. fired 223 rounds had casualties:- Killed — Gr. Fitzpatrick Wounded Sgt. Lovesey (remains at duty) Gr. Rowan. Gr. Connelly. Gr. Oliver. Gr. Wilson. Gr. Brown. Gr. Wiltshire. Br. Thorddin — missing — Lt. A. Cameron Gr. Gardner. Gr. Harvey. At 9.30 P.M. orders were received that Battys. were to be withdrawn — No notice — about 5 A.M. the enemy commenced a furious attack in the 4th Bty. were ordered to start gun fire	

Army Form C. 2118.

WAR DIARY
or
INTELLIGENCE SUMMARY.
(Erase heading not required.)

Instructions regarding War Diaries and Intelligence Summaries are contained in F.S. Regs., Part II. and the Staff Manual respectively. Title pages will be prepared in manuscript.

Hour, Date, Place	Summary of Events and Information	Remarks and references to Appendices
May 8th	10.30 P.M. Bty was ordered to 11 rounds. Ammunition was replenished during fire about 12.30 P.M. Teams were ridden in on arrival of this 400 m in Bty, whilst single guns were ammund'd to the guns. Between 1.P.M & 2.P.M. between Sgt. Reunion returned to the wagon line and came to bring out wagons & four gun teams out full. Between 4 & 5 P.M. we were again on the position emptied the wagon guns teams. He then came with the fire wagons & gun teams were in action, in turn one is return with 5 wagon loads of Ammun. but on arrival at their wagon line order was conveyed from Sgt. Reunion was ordered to take out the wagon teams only as the Bty was to be in bivouac. About 9 A.M. the 5th Bty. was heavily engaged & by about 10.30 A.M. orders were sent to the wagon line for Ammun. About 1.30 P.M. 4 wagons arrived close to the position but were not go up to the guns as they moved in to away, made the open 105th Bty. R.F.A. The teams indeed, ammg is seen fire, to be in bivouac 200 x further down the road under cover of some buildings + ammun. was carried up by hand. The teams at rest to the wagon line without casualty.	
May 9th	By 4 A.M. all ammn. carriages - horses and prisoners of war Bavarian (one wounded) had arrived at the wagon line. Reconnaissance was made during the day & that positions taken up at night as follows. 4th Bty. 200 x N.W. of Loek No 12. YPRES CANAL — 5th Bty, 400 x S.W. of YPRES LUNATIC ASYLUM — Bde. H.D. Qrs. moved to a point 500 x N. of VLAMERTINGHE — YPRES RD. +1000 x W. of YPRES.	
May 10th 11th	Btys. in action in same places but this no rounds.	
May 11th	4th Bty. in action in same place but this no rounds. This Bty was heavily shelled for four hours but only one casualty — Gr. Marlow slightly wounded	

(73989) W4141—463. 400,000. 9/14. H.&J.Ltd. Forms/C. 2118/10.

WAR DIARY or INTELLIGENCE SUMMARY.

Army Form C. 2118.

(Erase heading not required.)

Hour, Date, Place	Summary of Events and Information	Remarks and references to Appendices
May 11th	but he returned at 4 A.M. — 5th Bty. were at disposal of 27th Division. A reconnaissance was made during the day & a position alongside the Regt. just N. of the MENIN RD. & 2800 ft. E. of the centre of YPRES was reported by night. Capt. Harman being in command (Major Malony & horses were wounded while this Sect. was occupying the position.	
May 12th	Both Batty's in action in the same places. 4th Batty. fired N.E. rounds. 5th Batty. fired 8 rounds.	
May 13th	Batty's still in action in the same places. 4th Batty. fired N.E. rounds. About 4 P.M. the 4th D. Gs. were reoccupying trenches 1600 x in front of the Batty. forward section was mainly ruined & put out of their trenches — It. was seeing who was in the trenches as F.O.O. joined in a bayonet charge (himself killing three Germans with his revolver) and then on one covering being driven back he raced across in open [shell] under very heavy fire & succeeded in firing 202 rounds of the section on to the advancing enemy. The section fired on stopping the enemy between 8 P.M. and 9.30 P.M. & continually assisted the wagon look of horses. Horses were then sent to the wagon line two were wagon look of horses. This message was taken by Gr. Grosman on a bicycle who was not seen till the Summers arrived about 12.30 P.M. Remainder of the day was spent in the coming in to approximately former in position, they had a wonderful escape from machine gun fire as they were returning. Casualties — wounded. Gr. Wilfred. Gr. Stangster and Br. Doyle.
May 14th	4th Batty. still in action in the same place & the N.E. rounds. 5th Btty. still in action in the same place, during the night orders were received

Army Form C. 2118.

WAR DIARY
or
INTELLIGENCE SUMMARY.
(Erase heading not required.)

Instructions regarding War Diaries and Intelligence Summaries are contained in F. S. Regs., Part II. and the Staff Manual respectively. Title pages will be prepared in manuscript.

Hour, Date, Place	Summary of Events and Information	Remarks and references to Appendices
May 14th	The 5th Bty. were to return to the wagon line for a rest that this forward position was to be taken over by the 4th Bty. Capt. Anderson was reported missing. One of the running out. Proved to be nothing serious. Lt. G. Anman sent to hospital.	
May 16th	4th Bty. all day in action in same place. At 6 P.M. 4th Bty exp. to take up the forward action position from 5th Bty. until the presence of their exp. action. The night action carrying up a position two prepared during the day avoiding 300 yds E. of the crossroads of YPRES on bank of the moat. By 2.30 P.M. the — 5th Durham Bty. had manned the wagon line safely through their forward X. was staved as it came along the Rly. Capt. Anderson Lt. W. breaking movements through the day light to approach zone + manning stations etc. 6 O.C. advanced K. 4th Bty. The 4th Bty. fired 92 rounds that Night. casualties Bdr. H.O. Bro. moved to a house 500ft S.W. of YPRES.	
May 17th	4th Bty. in action in the same place. 5th Bty. still resting in wagon line. Bdr. Ho. Bro. moved to wagon line.	
May 18th	4th Bty. forward X. still in action in same place. Rear X. moved its position to our 100ft are E. of former one + 20ft S. of the MENIN RD. fired 93 rounds— 5th Bty. still in wagon line.	
May 19th	4th Bty. still in action in the same places. fired 33 rounds/ 1 Has casualties wounded Dr. Spence Dr. Hippell) 5th Bty. Present at disposal of 4th Division + put under orders of O.C. 32nd Bde. R.F.A. Reconnaissance made by Capt. K. Anderson + Bdr. Maj. R.M. Hutchinson. was made a position 500ft N. E. of YPRES + 400ft W. of LOCKS and YPRES CANAL. Position prepared during the night.	

(73989) W4141—463. 400,000. 9/14. H.&J.Ltd. Forms/C. 2118/M.

Army Form C. 2118.

WAR DIARY
or
INTELLIGENCE SUMMARY.
(Erase heading not required.)

Instructions regarding War Diaries and Intelligence Summaries are contained in F.S. Regs., Part II. and the Staff Manual respectively. Title pages will be prepared in manuscript.

Hour, Date, Place	Summary of Events and Information	Remarks and references to Appendices
May 20th	4th Bty. still in action in the same places. 2nd to 5th R.B. - 5th Bty. left wagon lines & occupied position they had previously prepared. Lt. G. Hixson returned from hospital at HAZEBROUCK.	
May 21st	4th & 5th Btys. still in action in same places this N.K. Kept rounds repeating	
May 22nd	" " " " " " " " " " " " " 50 "	"
May 23rd	" " " " " " " " " " " " " 16 & NIL "	"
May 24th	At 3. A.M. the enemy commenced a very violent attack by turning on gas & firing gas shells. The gas reached as far back as the wagon line although it caused considerable inconvenience then it did not put anyone out of action.	
	Narrative:- 4th Bty. At 3.10 A.M. enemy opened a very heavy forward X.R.	
3.20 A.M.	stunning section was badly gassed. At 3.30 A.M. forward X opened fire on invaders entombing trench mortar, Capt: J. Chapman having made his way up to forward X. was very soon there.	
3.30 A.M.	all telephone wires cut	
3.46 A.M.	communication established between forward X near X. by orderlies & rear X opened fire on same trench.	
4. A.M.	Telephone communication again obtained.	
4.30 A.M.	Enemy attack temporarily checked but wire again cut. No movement of any numerous attempts failed to restore telephonic communication.	
5. A.M.	Enemy again advanced more strongly aided.	

Army Form C. 2118.

WAR DIARY
or
INTELLIGENCE SUMMARY.
(Erase heading not required.)

Instructions regarding War Diaries and Intelligence Summaries are contained in F.S. Regs., Part II. and the Staff Manual respectively. Title pages will be prepared in manuscript.

Hour, Date, Place	Summary of Events and Information	Remarks and references to Appendices
May 24th		
9. A.M.	At 8 A.M. near X sent an orderly to forward X for orders & was told to watch MENIN RD. & send for more ammn.	
9.30 A.M.	Enemy ammn track N. of Rly. & our infty. re-occupied their front trenches.	
10 A.M. to 11.30 A.M.	Rear X. ordered not to fire N. of Rly., & only fire when nonnees could be observed. Forward X under very heavy shell fire, infants reld. from movement that were advancing S. of MENIN RD. Observation and not continue owing to receiving fire was directed on an between RAILWAY & BELLEWAARD LAKE. Annoying fire from 6 men at No. 2. ammn were removed out by our three bt. no very severe movements. The detachment was made up by replacements & men from other guns. A small number of men were seen crossing MENIN RD. from S.W. they were sacrificed as our own.	
12 Noon	Fire was ceased owing to shortage of ammn.	
12.30 P.M.		
1.15 P.M.	Fire opened from No. 1. gun only on men N.E of BELLEWAARD LAKE. No. 2 gun could not be mounted owing to it being too heavy.	
2. P.M.	All ammn. with forward X having been expended his officer in chge. sent for provisions replenishment it was decided to retire on rear X. All ranks including wounded moved near X we cannot further own. Saints ammn tracks were brought back with prisoners.	
2.40 P.M.	Rear X. was massed, orders were there found for withdrawal of forward X to wagon line. Personnel of forward X & an ammo. gun of rear X was not back to wagon line. A spare rail of fire was then continued on ane N. of HOOGE & E. of BELLEWAARD LAKE from the remaining gun.	

(73989) W4141—463. 400,000. 9/14. H.&J. Ltd. Forms/C. 2118/10.

WAR DIARY
or
INTELLIGENCE SUMMARY.
(Erase heading not required.)

Army Form C. 2118.

Instructions regarding War Diaries and Intelligence Summaries are contained in F.S. Regs., Part II. and the Staff Manual respectively. Title pages will be prepared in manuscript.

Hour, Date, Place	Summary of Events and Information	Remarks and references to Appendices
May 24th 4.15 P.M.	Runners bring an approved position was reported to Bn. Maj. 17th D. weavon who sent orders that guns of forward X were to be withdrawn at night, one to rejoin near X, six guns to return to wagon line. This was successfully accomplished by Capt. Chapman by 11.40 P.M. he was every anxious as Sgt. Ward Ash. He later receiving a wound through his cap + another through his collar but he was unengaged. Casualties – Runners Gr. Chapman (since dead) Gr. Smeltie – Powell – Maran – Steuaman – 2nd Cue – Palin – Rimmer – Sgt. Hall. The later remaining at ashep. Runners here too. [An account of the day's operations has been forwarded to C.R.A. 29th Div. (whose whereabouts commanding this Bty. was.) + to C R A 50th Northumbrian Div. Special mention being made of the good work of Capt. C.L. Chapman – Lt. E. Darling – B.Q.M. Sergt. Thomas Dr. Sergt. Smith – Corrie. also of the puckey action of Lt. E. Scott R.A.M.C.T who remained all day with 2nd Vaughan 3rd Royal Fusiliers who was mortally wounded – where he carried over a mile under fire at night to a dressing station. Sir Darling Att. 3. Atty. a strong enemy attack encured by gas began to envelope.	
3.15 A.M.	Battery opened heavy enemy Countries N + S. of SHELLTRAP FARM. Two strewing stations were used Lt. M. Murray working from one on the night report. F. Andrew from one on the left. Telephone wires were entirely cut. his messages received this time onwards communications were made by the B.C. (Capt. V. Andrew) nothing forward coming back with comprehensive.	
11.15 A.M.	Information was received that emergency guns in provision of SHELLTRAP FARM and orders were given to limber up on the area N. E. of said farm in preparation for a counter attack.	

Army Form C. 2118.

WAR DIARY
or
INTELLIGENCE SUMMARY.
(Erase heading not required.)

Instructions regarding War Diaries and Intelligence Summaries are contained in F.S. Regs., Part II. and the Staff Manual respectively. Title pages will be prepared in manuscript.

Hour, Date, Place	Summary of Events and Information	Remarks and references to Appendices
May 24th 1 P.M.	Orders were received to increase rate of fire.	
1.45 P.M.	Fire was stopped to enable the counter attack to be launched. The barricades refused fire to bear been very effective.	
2.30 P.M.	Enemy outposts were located in Farms 200ft N. of WIELTJE and 1500 E. of the same place. Fire was turned on these.	
6.30 P.M.	No.1 Gun fired army fire minm, at SHELLTRAP FARM. as our infantry were unable to walk an attack at 10.30. P.M.	
6.30 P.M.	Orders were received to cease fire minmense to the W. side of the YPRES CANAL to the position occupied by the 4th Brig. from Hay 19th this was accomplished without casualty. Although this immediate vicinity was under shell fire most of the day the actual position of the guns does not appear to have been located. Number of rounds fired 338.	
May 25th	4th Bty. in action in the same place. fired 22 rounds. No.1 Gun fired 16 rounds Bde. Lieson.	
	I.O.M. 5th Corps for repairs. Casualties - wounded Pt. Wilson.	
	5th Bty. in action in the same place fired 16 rounds.	
May 26th	Btys. in action in the same places. No rounds fired.	
May 27th	Btys. " " " " " 4th fired 6 rounds. 5th fired N.I.L. but had casualties - wounded Gr. Whittaker Pt. Fraser.	
May 28th	Btys. still in action in the same places. Reconnaissances made + positions further in rear selected considerable work done on improving dugouts systems. Btys. both fired NIL rounds.	

WAR DIARY
or
INTELLIGENCE SUMMARY.
(Erase heading not required.)

Army Form C. 2118.

Hour, Date, Place	Summary of Events and Information	Remarks and references to Appendices
May 29th	Both Batys. still in action in the same place. Fired 8 + 3 rounds respectively. During the night 28th - 29th Lt-G. Allison had the horse ambulance under him while passing through YPRES. The following was received:— "OC. 2nd Durham Bay R.F.A.T.F. — RA. 168. 29/5/15. The G.O.C. is asked to convey to all ranks of your Bty, his keen appreciation of the work done by them during the recent fighting, work which was carried out under very trying and arduous conditions A.F.A. 27th (R) minimal Allison "	
May 30th	Batys. still in action in the same place. Fired 17 + 6 rounds respectively.	
May 31st	Batys. " " " " " " " " 8 + Nil " "	4th Bty. became attached to 3rd Div. an army corps ran from 27th. Quite a number of H.E. shells fired aerial near to the horse lines through which a number of horses were picked up in various parts of the lines. No damage was done.
June 1st	Batys. in action in the same place. Fired 2 + Nil rounds respectively.	
June 2nd	" " " " " " " " " 10 + 11 " "	4th Bty. H.Q. line and MENIN ROAD adjoining were heavily shelled from 2.30 P.M. to 5.30 P.M. an telephone wires cut but no other damage. Wires are repaired by 8 P.M.
June 3rd	Batys. in action in same place fired 10 + Nil rounds respectively.	
June 4th	Batys. " " " " " " " " Nil + 4 " " . One gun of 4th Bty. occupied a position which had been prepared night of June 3rd on bank of moat round YPRES near ECOLE d'EQUITATION. This Batys. (No.2a) was unlike by Lt. Gen. Sir H. Hunning K.C.B., & Maj. Gen. Brown (Actg. Comm. to 5th Corps)	

Army Form C. 2118.

WAR DIARY
or
INTELLIGENCE SUMMARY.
(Erase heading not required.)

Instructions regarding War Diaries and Intelligence Summaries are contained in F.S. Regs., Part II. and the Staff Manual respectively. Title pages will be prepared in manuscript.

Hour, Date, Place	Summary of Events and Information	Remarks and references to Appendices
June 5th	4th Bty. in action in same place, fired 14 rounds. 5th Bty.(D) continued to commence of 50th wagon. Sent in order to 4th Bty.(D) when when it should only have returned to wagon line. C.P.A. and O.C. Bty. made a reconnaissance for a position for the Bty. to come in unfit, of its own Division. A position was selected 400' N.W. of ETANG DE ZILLEBEKE.	
June 6th	4th Bty. still in action in same place, fired 14 rounds. 5th Bty. preparing position.	
June 7th	4th Bty. still in action in same place, fired 14 rounds. 5th Bty. orders to new position. Bde. H.Q. Bde. moved to ESTAMINET LA PLAIN D'EXERCISE. Lt. Col. A.W. SILLERY, appointed nominal C.R.A. 50th Division. 5th Bty. had not arrived when H.E. arrived close to him at 1 P.M. but sustained no casualty.	
June 8th	4th Btys. still in action in same place, fired 15 rounds respectively. Bde. H.Q. Bde. moved to ÉCOLE DE BIENFAISANCE E. of YPRES. Heavy bombardment in the afternoon interfered with our telephonic communications.	
June 9th	Btys. in action in same place, fired 20 nil rounds respectively.	
June 10th	" " " " " " "	NIL NIL
June 11th	" " " " " " "	
June 12th	" " " " " " "	24+18
	Received that Bty's H.Q. must have an telephone line in triplicate this was done nightly during the night 12th/13th.	Orders

(73989) W.4141—463. 400,000. 9/14. H.& J. Ltd. Forms/C. 2118/10.

Army Form C. 2118.

WAR DIARY
or
INTELLIGENCE SUMMARY.
(Erase heading not required.)

Instructions regarding War Diaries and Intelligence Summaries are contained in F. S. Regs., Part II. and the Staff Manual respectively. Title pages will be prepared in manuscript.

Hour, Date, Place	Summary of Events and Information	Remarks and references to Appendices
June 13th	Batys. still in action in the same places, fired 9 + 1 rounds respectively. The non X of WM Batty, and one gun of the 5th Batty, joined in forward X. of WM Batty, are now under command of Major R. Chapman.	
June 14th	Batys. in action in the same places, fired NIL and 18 rounds respectively. Capt Washburn Lt. Hallam were sent to the Bde. for duty from the 4th South Midland Bde. R.H.A. T.F.	
June 15th	Batys. in action in the same places, fired 52 + NIL rounds respectively.	
June 16th	4th Battery still in action in the same place. 5th Bty " " " " " On this day a concerted attack was made on the enemy's trenches from Railway Wood on the N to Hooge on the S. The attack opened at 2.50 A.M. each unit being allotted about 5 mins to change registration. The bombardment proper started at 3.20 A.M. until two pauses at 3.40 A.M. and 4 A.M. At 4.15 A.M. the artillery lifted to the 2nd line of enemy trenches, the infantry attack being launched at that time on to the enemy's first line. This line of defence was found to have been completely destroyed – wire entanglements, trenches, emplacements, everything being completely demolished, the thoroughness of the destruction led to our infantry advance being much too rapidly with the result that they became disorganised + rushing forward got into the zone of our artillery fire. Fire was then lifted as a further objective let the infantry, instead of trying to consolidate the ground won that they had gained by this time, again rushed forward. At 9.35 A.M. a report was received that Liverpool Scottish had captured the strong trench which we hoped BELLEWAARDE FARM. At 9.45 A.M. enemy counter attacks commenced	

Army Form C. 2118.

WAR DIARY
or
INTELLIGENCE SUMMARY.
(Erase heading not required.)

Instructions regarding War Diaries and Intelligence Summaries are contained in F.S. Regs., Part II. and the Staff Manual respectively. Title pages will be prepared in manuscript.

Hour, Date, Place	Summary of Events and Information	Remarks and references to Appendices
10. A.M.	to envelope.	
10.8. A.M.	A report was received from F.O.O. that our Infty. were falling back through Y wood.	
	We commenced fresh attack on Y. wood, Swans heard to have figures at S. end of this wood.	
10.15. A.M.	C. Oc. 9in Infty. Bde. sent a message "Counter attack is taking place on Y. wood, please open fire at once" — No definite information being obtainable no action was taken.	
10.27. A.M.	Opened fire on DEADMANS BOTTOM.	
10.35 A.M.	Brans refused to open fire on this objective but this was not done as F.O.O. reported it too dangerous for our own Infty.	
12. NOON.	401 rounds had been expended.	
1.55 P.M.	Two wagon loads ammun. arrived safely.	
2.30 P.M.	3 or 4 wagy explosions reported to have taken place in DEADMANSBOTTOM as result of our 5"Hour. H.E. creep were firing by many into Y. wood.	
2.55 P.M.	Enemy lifted his fire into our original front line trenches.	
3.5 P.M.	Three wagon loads of Ammun. arrived safely.	
4.15 P.M.	A slow rate of fire was opened on DEADMANS BOTTOM.	
7.20 to 7.45 P.M.	Enemy opened heavy fire on our front line & G.H.Q.lines.	
8. P.M.	Night rounds laid out, to cover 150ˣ in front of our front line.	
	Capt. C. L. Chapman was recommended for an D.S.O. for his persistent work as F.O.O. & also in many valuable & accurate reports of the enemy's own movements. No 650 g. of Saunders was also recommended for the D.C.M. for his	

(73989) W4141—463. 400,000. 9/14. H.&J.Ltd. Forms/C. 2118/10.

WAR DIARY
or
INTELLIGENCE SUMMARY.

(Erase heading not required.)

Army Form C. 2118.

Hour, Date, Place	Summary of Events and Information	Remarks and references to Appendices
June 17th	excellent work on trenches. — No 1215 G.T. complete of the Bde. was ammunition reconnoitred. Bdy. fired 547 rounds. 5th Bdy. had a most trying night in the zone of action.	
June 18th	Both Btys. still in action in the same places, neither fired any rounds, but the Bdy. was mainly shelled at 8·4 P.M. Sustained casualties — wounded one man (sergeant) and one gun went badly downward.	
June 19th	Both Bttys. in action in the same places, fired 12+10 rounds respectively. NIL +17 " " OC +9th	
June 20th	Bde. R.T.A. + O.C. "C" Btty, 4th Bde. arrived at Bde. Hd. Qrs. to arrange support infantry, the 4th in having men ordered to take over from our own line.	
	Both Bttys. in action in the same places, fired 35+9 rounds respectively. At 11:5 P.M. a message was received from Brig. Gent. Cmdg. 8th Infty. Bde. to bring many guns to bear on DEADMANS BOTTOM. Night times of the Bdy. having been laid on this spot a rapid fire was opened at once.	
1:40 A.M.	a message was received from 8" Infty. Bde. asking for fire to "cease to be opened".	
2:25 A.M.	All telephonic communication cut.	
2:30 A.M.	fire was re-opened on the same objective a message having been brought by hand by Lt. G. Gibson R.T.A.	
2:40 A.M.	cease fire	
3:40 A.M.	Telephonic communication with 8th Infty. Bde. re-established.	
4:20 A.M.	all quiet again.	
9:40 P.M.	Rt. X. of 4th Bdy. withdrawn to wagon line its place being taken by a X of "C" Bdy. 4·9" Bde. R.T.A.	

WAR DIARY
or
INTELLIGENCE SUMMARY.
(Erase heading not required.)

Army Form C. 2118.

Instructions regarding War Diaries and Intelligence Summaries are contained in F.S. Regs., Part II. and the Staff Manual respectively. Title pages will be prepared in manuscript.

Hour, Date, Place	Summary of Events and Information	Remarks and references to Appendices
June 22nd	5ᵗʰ Bty. tk of position in action in same place, left X of 4ᵗʰ Bty, whereupon in its place taking up a X of "C" Bty, 4ᵗʰ Bty. Bde. R.A. — Bde. H.Q. Bn. moved from ECOLE DE BIENFAISANCE to wagon line. 4ᵗʰ Bty. returning to wagon line. 5ᵗʰ Bty. still in action in same place.	
June 23rd	Bde. H.Q. ra. — Bty. & Ammun. Col. moved to a point S. of KEMMEL HILL. Bde. H.Q. ra. occupied their permanent position. The Bde. Ammun. Col. also occupied its permanent position 1500' S.W. of LOCRE on the LOCRE-BAILLEUL RD. 4ᵗʰ Bty occupied position as follows: Rt X 1700' N. of NEUVE EGLISE VILLAGE in left X 2000' N. of KEMMEL HILL. 5ᵗʰ Bty left its position went into old wagon line at VLAMERTINGHE.	
June 24th	4ᵗʰ Bty. return still in action in the same place. 5ᵗʰ Bty. moved from its lines at VLAMERTINGHE & went into temporary lines into Ammun. Col.	
June 25th	4ᵗʰ Bty. left X rejoined their Rt X. 5ᵗʰ Bty came into action in place of 4ᵗʰ Bty. left X. 4ᵗʰ Bty. fired 25 rounds.	
June 26th	Bty's in action in same place fired NIL no rounds repeatedly	26 rnds
June 27th	" " " " " " " " " " " "	10 +2 "
June 28th	" " " " " " " " " " " "	NIL "
June 29th	" " " " " " " " " " " "	NIL "
June 30th / July 1st	" " " " " " " " " " " "	NIL + 5 rounds

Army Form C. 2118.

WAR DIARY
or
INTELLIGENCE SUMMARY.
(Erase heading not required.)

Instructions regarding War Diaries and Intelligence Summaries are contained in F.S. Regs., Part II. and the Staff Manual respectively. Title pages will be prepared in manuscript.

Hour, Date, Place	Summary of Events and Information	Remarks and references to Appendices
July 2nd	Btty's in action in the same places, fired 23 rounds of repetiring. Lt E Darling was wounded in three places while returning from the trenches, he was sent to H.Q. at BAILLEUL.	
July 3rd	Btty's in action in the same places, fired 9 rnds rounds repetiring.	
July 4th	" " " " " " " " NIL+20 "	
July 5th	" " " " " " " " NIL "	
July 6th	" " " " " " " " NIL "	
July 7th	" " " " " " " " 23+15 "	
July 8th	" " " " " " " " NIL+19 "	
July 9th	" " " " " " " " 6 +NIL "	
July 10th	" " " " " " " " 55 +NIL " during night of 9th/10th our Btty fired at various points at known or various in German lines said to be a mine. This was done at request of Canadian Division. My own & our S.O.C. was concerned - g.s. Poelcapelle Vivirion telephones wounded whilst returning wire between Batt'y g'ps & trenches.	
July 11th	Btty's in action in the same places - fired 12 rpo rds. repetiring with Btty.	
July 12th	Btty's in action in the same places fired NIL rounds each.	
July 13th	" " " " " " " " 7 + NIL rounds repetiring	
July 14th	" " " " " " " " NIL+0 "	
July 15th	" " " " " " " " 24 +NIL " Lt. Ricciardi joined 4th Btty. for duty.	

WAR DIARY
or
INTELLIGENCE SUMMARY.
(Erase heading not required.)

Army Form C. 2118.

Instructions regarding War Diaries and Intelligence Summaries are contained in F.S. Regs. Part II and the Staff Manual respectively. Title pages will be prepared in manuscript.

Hour, Date, Place	Summary of Events and Information	Remarks and references to Appendices
July 16th	Battys in action in the same places fired 6 & nil rounds respectively. 4th Batty had casualties - Bomr Connell & Dvr Shadwick killed & Dvr Blenman wounded, all telephonists, being struck by a rifle grenade in the trenches.	
July 17th	Battys in action in the same places, fired 14 nil rounds respectively. One section of the 5th Battery came out of action, moved to temporary wagon line at farm 750 yds N of Nieppe.	
July 18th	Battys in action in the same places, fired nil & 5 rounds respectively. Headquarter Staff, 4th Battery remaining section & 5th Battery came out of action at 10 pm moved into the wagon line at the Park, Armentières, with the exception of the section of the 5th Battery which proceeded direct to the gun position at a point close to the Rue Eyt between Houplines & Nivel Houplines where the other section was already in position. The Ammunition Column moved at 4 pm & proceeded to the wagon line just mentioned.	
July 19th	5th Battery in same position fired 19 rounds.	
July 20th	" " " " fired 12 " 4th Battery, right section, moved into position close to - mile E. of the Church at la Chapelle D'Armentières.	
July 21st	Battys in same positions fired 17 & 8 rounds respectively. The 4th Battery left section moved into position beside right section.	
July 22nd	Battys in same positions, fired 12 & nil rounds respectively.	
July 23rd	" " " " " 7 & 10 " "	
July 24th	" " " " " 16 & 9 " "	
July 25th	" " " " " 27 & NIL " "	
July 26th	" " " " " 32 & NIL " "	
July 27th	" " " " " NIL & 9 " "	
July 28th	" " " " " 8 & NIL " "	
July 29th	" " " " " NIL & NIL " "	
July 30th	" " " " " NIL & 7 = 111 " "	

12/6650

ar
a96

30=/5 Kirurim

1/4 år kontrakt for Bde R+A.
Bot II
Fra 1-31.8.15

Army Form C. 2118.

4th Northumbrian (How.) Brigade R.F.A. T.F.

WAR DIARY
or
INTELLIGENCE SUMMARY.
(Erase heading not required.)

Instructions regarding War Diaries and Intelligence Summaries are contained in F. S. Regs., Part II. and the Staff Manual respectively. Title pages will be prepared in manuscript.

Hour, Date, Place	Summary of Events and Information	Remarks and references to Appendices
August 1st	Btys. still in action in the same places fired 14 + 4 rounds respectively	
2nd	" Nil + Nil "	
3rd	" 13 " 12 "	
4th	" Nil " 12 "	
5th	" 10 " Nil "	
6th	" Nil " Nil "	
7th	" 9 " Nil "	
8th	" 16 " Nil "	
9th	" Nil " 7 Nil "	
10th	" 3 " 14 "	
11th	" 22 " Nil "	
12th	" Nil " Nil "	
13th	" 12 " 11 "	
14th	" Nil " Nil "	
15th	" 28 " 6 "	
16th	" 3 " Nil "	
17th	" Nil " 14 "	
18th	" Nil " Nil "	
19th	" 28 " 20 "	
20th	Hooplines was rather heavily shelled by the enemy a railway + aerodrome were set on fire. 20 " 26	
21st	" 10 " Nil	
22nd	" Nil " Nil	
23rd	" Nil " 4	

Army Form C. 2118.

4th Yorkshire (How) Brigade R.F.A.T.F.

WAR DIARY
or
INTELLIGENCE SUMMARY.
(Erase heading not required.)

Instructions regarding War Diaries and Intelligence Summaries are contained in F. S. Regs., Part II. and the Staff Manual respectively. Title pages will be prepared in manuscript.

Hour, Date, Place	Summary of Events and Information	Remarks and references to Appendices
August 24th	Both Batteries in action in the same places fired 1 Nil rounds respectively.	
25th	" " " " " " " 6 20 "	
26th	" " " " " " " 6 Nil "	
27th	" " " " " " " Nil Nil "	
28th	" " " " " " " 12 4 "	
29th	" " " " " " " Nil + 19 "	
30th	" " " " " " " 20 + Nil "	
31st	" " " " " " " Nil + 13 "	

50

1/2 Nbrn Bde R FA
Am Col

Vol XII

121/7051

50th Division

4th Northumbrian Bde R.F.A.

Vol III

Sep 15

4 Northumbrian (How) Brigade RFA T.F.

WAR DIARY
or
INTELLIGENCE SUMMARY.
(Erase heading not required.)

Army Form C. 2118.

Hour, Date, Place	Summary of Events and Information	Remarks and references to Appendices
1915 Sept 1st	Both Batteries in action on the same places fired 15 + 15 rounds respectively	
2nd	" " " " " NIL + 4 " "	
3rd	" " " " " " " "	
4th	" " " " " 14 + NIL " "	
5th	2nd Lieut W. J. McCallum joined 5th Battery for duty	
6th	Both Batteries in action on the same place fired 48 + 4 " "	
7th	" " " " " NIL + 8 " "	
	" " " " " 9 + 4 " "	
	" " " " " 6 + NIL " "	
8th	Bombr. W.B. Couper, telephonist, 5th Battery wounded by bullet in the leg.	
9th	Both Batteries in action on the same places fired NIL + 18 rounds respectively	
10th	" " " " " 2 + NIL " "	
11th	" " " " " 16 + 12 " "	
12th	" " " " " 19 + 22 " "	
13th	2nd Lieut W.J. McCallum sent to Hospital suffering from Mumps.	
14th	Both Batteries in action on the same places fired 9 + NIL rounds respectively	
15th	" " " " " 22 + 28 " "	
16th	" " " " " 8 + 6 " "	
17th	" " " " " 14 + 6 " "	
18th	" " " " " 18 + NIL " "	
19th	" " " " " 11 + NIL " "	
20th	" " " " " 15 + NIL " "	
21st	Small bombardment of enemy's "Black Redoubt"	
	2nd Lieut F.H.N. Hegel joined Ammunition Column for duty.	
	Both Batteries in action on the same places fired 9 + 8 rounds respectively	
22nd	" " " " " 2 + 10 " "	
23rd	" " " " " 19 + 20 " "	
24th	" " " " " NIL + 5 " "	
25th	2nd Lieut W.A. Dearham joined for duty was posted to Ammunition Column.	
	In conjunction with operations to the North & South a feint attack proceeded by smoke was commenced at 5 am. by heavy artillery fire which lasted until 6.5 am. This produced no retaliation whatever from the Germans who doubtless realised that the attack was but a feint. After 6.5 am the rest of the day was quiet.	

4th NORTHUMBRIAN HOW. BDE. R.F.A.

WAR DIARY
or
INTELLIGENCE SUMMARY.
(Erase heading not required.)

Army Form C. 2118.

Hour, Date, Place	Summary of Events and Information	Remarks and references to Appendices
1915		
Sept. 25th	Both Batteries in action in the same places fired 82 . 81 rounds respectively	
" 26th	" " " " " " 6 . 8 " "	
" 27th	" " " " " " 17 . 23 " "	
" 28th	" " " " " " NIL. NIL " "	
" 29th	" " " " " " 4 . NIL " "	
" 30th	" " " " " " NIL . 10 " "	

Ayjockey

50th Division

1/4th Northumberland Fusiliers Bde

Oct. 1915.

Vol IV

121/7437

Army Form C. 2118

4th NORTHUMBRIAN HOW. BDE. R.F.A.

WAR DIARY
or
INTELLIGENCE SUMMARY

(Erase heading not required.)

Instructions regarding War Diaries and Intelligence Summaries are contained in F. S. Regs., Part II. and the Staff Manual respectively. Title Pages will be prepared in manuscript.

Place	Date	Hour	Summary of Events and Information	Remarks and references to Appendices
Armentières	1.10.15		Both Batteries in action in the same places. Fired NIL , 10 rounds respectively	
	2.10.15		" " " " " " " " NIL , 4 " "	
	3.10.15		" " " " " " " " 8 , NIL " "	
	4.10.15		" " " " " " " " 19 , NIL " "	
	5.10.15		" " " " " " " " NIL , NIL " "	
	6.10.15		" " " " " " " " NIL , 20 " "	
	7.10.15		" " " " " " " " 9 , 12 " "	
	8.10.15		" " " " " " " " NIL , NIL " "	
	9.10.15		" " " " " " " " 18 , NIL " "	
	10.10.15		" " " " " " " " 13 , 6 " "	
	11.10.15		" " " " " " " " 11 , 15 " "	
	12.10.15		" " " " " " " "	
	13.10.15	2 p.m.	A smoke & artillery demonstration took place all along the line Both Batteries in action in the same places. Fired 36 , 24 rounds respectively	
	14.10.15		" " " " " " " " 6 , NIL " "	
	15.10.15		" " " " " " " " 6 , 4 " "	
	16.10.15		" " " " " " " " 6 , 6 " "	
	17.10.15		" " " " " " " " 4 , 4 " "	
	18.10.15		" " " " " " " " 7 , 8 " "	
	19.10.15		" " " " " " " " 9 , NIL " "	
	20.10.15		" " " " " " " " 2 , 4 " "	
	21.10.15		" " " " " " " " 12 , NIL " "	
	22.10.15	9 a.m.	On this day we fired the forty pound shell for the first time. After nightfall one section of the 4th Battery & one section of the 5th Battery were withdrawn to the Wagon line their places being taken by sections of the 97th Brigade R.F.A., 21st Division. The section of the 4th Battery & the section of the 5th Battery which had been withdrawn from action together with the Ammunition Column less two Wagons moved off to new positions near Hazebrouck	
	23.10.15		The remaining sections of the Batteries in the same positions. Fired 18 , 18 rounds respectively After nightfall the remaining section of each battery was withdrawn to the 2 , 3 Wagon line, the places being taken by the 97th Brigade R.F.A. 21st Division	

(B 11875) W. W. 593/826 1,000,000 4/15 J.B.C. & A. A.D.S.S./Forms/C. 2118.

Army Form C. 2118

4th NORTHUMBRIAN HOW. BDE. R.F.A.

WAR DIARY
or
INTELLIGENCE SUMMARY
(Erase heading not required.)

Instructions regarding War Diaries and Intelligence Summaries are contained in F. S. Regs., Part II. and the Staff Manual respectively. Title Pages will be prepared in manuscript.

Place	Date	Hour	Summary of Events and Information	Remarks and references to Appendices
Armentières	24.10.15	9 am	Headquarters Staff, the remaining section of each Battery the remaining two wagons of ammunition	
		4.30 pm	Column moved off from Wagon Line. Arrived at new position round Hazebrouck - Mondefour road. Headquarters V.15, 5th Battery V.15, 4th Battery V.16. Ammunition Column V.21. Reference Belgium & France Sheet 27 (1:40,000).	
W. Hazebrouck	25.10.15		Brigade at rest	
	26.10.15		do. Colonel & Battery Commanders went up to reconnoitre new positions in neighbourhood of La Chapelle d'Armentières and Bois Grenier.	
	27.10.15		Brigade at rest.	
	28.10.15		do	
	29.10.15		do	
	30.10.15		do	
	31.10.15		do	

A. Younghusband
Col. L. Northns. How. Bde. R.F.A. T.F.

50th Division

1/4th Manchester Bde R.F.A.

121/7730

Army Form C. 2118

4th NORTHUMBRIAN HOW. BDE. R.F.A.

WAR DIARY
or
INTELLIGENCE SUMMARY
(Erase heading not required.)

Instructions regarding War Diaries and Intelligence Summaries are contained in F. S. Regs., Part II. and the Staff Manual respectively. Title Pages will be prepared in manuscript.

Place	Date	Hour	Summary of Events and Information	Remarks and references to Appendices
[illegible]	1/11/15		Fatigue parties from each Battery consisting of 20 men van officer went to La Chapelle d'Armentières & Bois Grenier respectively to prepare gun positions. Brigade at rest.	
	2.11.15 to 8.11.15		Brigade at rest.	
Nr Caestre	9.11.15		Brigade moved into new rest billets near Caestre. The units moved separately & were in their new billets by noon. Positions - Headquarters Staff W.2.d.1.9.; 4th Battery W.2.d.3.0.; 5th Battery W.3.d.2.2.; Ammunition Column W.2.c.4.1. Reference Sheet 27.	
	9.11.15 to 12.11.15		Brigade at rest.	
	13.11.15		Fatigue parties returned from La Chapelle d'Armentières & Bois Grenier	
	13.11.15 to 18.11.15		Brigade at rest.	
	19.11.15		2nd Lieut R. A. Watson joined as additional officer for instruction was posted to 5th (How) Battery	
	19.11.15 to 20.11.15		Brigade at rest.	
	21.11.15		After Church Parade Brig-Gen Newshaw, C.R.A., presented Gr. J. Rambrooks with the Croix de Guerre, awarded to him for distinguished conduct with regard to telephones near Ypres	
	22.11.15 to 30.11.15		Brigade at rest.	

[signature]
Lieut. Col. R.A.
Commdg. 4th North'n How. Bde. R.F.A. (T.F.)

1/4th Nantawnian Bde (Hons) RFA

Dec / vol VI

50.

WAR DIARY or INTELLIGENCE SUMMARY

Army Form C. 2118

4th NORTHUMBRIAN HOW. BDE. R.F.A.

Place	Date	Hour	Summary of Events and Information	Remarks and references to Appendices
Var Casche	1/10/15		Brigade at rest	
	3/11/15		Brigade (less Amm. Col.) moved to 2nd Army Training Area at Lederzule was killed near Ledergule	
	6/11/15			
	7/11/15		Brigade at Training Area	
	16/11/15		Brigade returned to Bat Sticks at Caestre	
	17/11/15		Brigade relieving Col Stockley Re 2 Battery Comdrs and Adjutant accompanied by OC's and O's of 1st 2nd & 3rd Lat Bdes RFA went by motor to reconnoitre the Bde Hdqs RA 9 & Div at Hooggraaf. Posn also red the CRA 9th Division. Later Col Stockley the 2 BC's and Adjutant walked round the trenches for positions with Col Ritchie RA 9th Division. Capt Anderson was left from his to wait with the Battery. on 5th Battery was to relieve. Col Stockley Major Chalmer and Adjt accompanied by Col Ritchie went on to find a position for the 4 Battery. The suggested position was found quite unsuitable & further reconnaissance was made and position for 1st 2 guns was chosen. Also trouble against a part that of work by Lt Sim for use. A bed	
	18/11/15		of horses required. Bury left with Col Ritchie	

4th Northumbrian How. Bde. R.F.A.

WAR DIARY
or
INTELLIGENCE SUMMARY

Army Form C. 2118

Place	Date	Hour	Summary of Events and Information	Remarks and references to Appendices
	18/4/15		On reporting to R.A H.Q. 50 Div. a full report on the situation was made to B. R.A.	
	19/4/15		Before our Col marched to join Major Lewis, march been delayed on account of enemy fire attack.	
	–/4/15		4 & 5th Batteries out Alright on in Major Lewis OC Bde and Divnl Off met Advgd party. Bde H.Q. entering about 3 P.M. Alphonsine received the Br H.Q 9 Div. No 1 C 55 Bty would be shelled by enemy at Briyser. Telegram No 3. and Br H/H 9 Div. that enemy supplied could not be carried out. 5th Battery stood in 2 lines. Off to serve 4 Heavy? Carbellon 5 55 & shrap. ep read to 6.05 R. Smith in 54 C 9 Brid in so oper 3 Brown in 54 A/4 & Gny 2 Wounded to sly for Smithing both 3 Batty of Lynch wounded (on duty) 4 Battery Lieut (?illegible) and Cadet Liubrandin & Sweloren for 2 June.	4/F unknown checked
	20/4/15		Situation record from BMFA 9 Div that C 55 Bty arrived at all with recent of Wednesday 2 stood but ? to bear 5th Battery fell in reserve to June – in Carvallier.	

WAR DIARY or INTELLIGENCE SUMMARY

Army Form C. 2118

4th NORTHUMBRIAN HOW. Bde. R.F.A.

Place	Date	Hour	Summary of Events and Information	Remarks and references to Appendices
	2/4/15		"A" Battery fired 7 rounds. O.C. Bde. had interview with O.C. C.53 Bty. & arranged for the handing over of all their Sections wire to 4th Bty.	
	23/4/15		12 rounds. Lt. Strathy and Capt. Chapman went out to reconnoitre for further positions. O/ 10 a.m. C.53 Bty. was handed over to Command of O.C. 4th Bde with orders from R.A. of 1st Div. that Bty. was to be withdrawn this afternoon. O.C. 4th Bty. had lunch with. Information – Wolthus wires from C.53 R.A. 50th Div. fully informed over telephone as to the Zwertjes ferry is in a position to cover left of Div. Zone. Bty. received from Staff Capt. R.A. 50th Div. about 12 noon that C.R.A., B.M. were fully aware of the situation. C.53. confirmed this wire at 2.30 P.M. C.R.A. 50th Div. at H.Q. 4th North Bde. at about 3.30 P.M. 4th Battery took in 2 guns at 12 M.M. C.R.A. 50th Div. arrived 100 m. and walked 5.1 Bty position with O.C. Bde. O/ 10.20 a.m. Instructions received over phone from O.C. A.S.C. that battery system of drawing rations was to be modified in lieu of present system of drawing by Bde. O/ 12.40 Staff Capt. R.A. 50th Div. roused up by messenger from Army Corps to be informed that G.5.1 Battery 20-3 guns were wished and left to 4th Battery 2 guns were in position but not injected. Position Vlillure Comm. established with 4th Battery about 12 noon.	

Army Form C. 2118.

4th NORTHUMBRIAN HOW. BDE. R.F.A.

WAR DIARY
or
INTELLIGENCE SUMMARY
(Erase heading not required.)

Instructions regarding War Diaries and Intelligence Summaries are contained in F. S. Regs., Part II. and the Staff Manual respectively. Title Pages will be prepared in manuscript.

Place	Date	Hour	Summary of Events and Information	Remarks and references to Appendices
	27/4/15		Telephone communication with 5" Battery was not possible except over the line of the 1st Bde R.F.A. Major Rappler Wounded from Lieut. Howard W.A. Robinson newly appointed CRA 50th Div. called with Gen Hurshaw at 4th Bde HQ about 10.30. The gun positions were pointed out to him on map by OC Bde. 5" Battery continued registering. 763 Lt Henry J. was wounded by rifle bullet while at Wagon Line at 10.35 P.M.	
	27/4/15		4" Battery fired 11 rounds. 5" " " 7 " Both Batteries continued registering. OC Bde & OC 4" Battery continued their search for positions for remaining section of 4" Battery without success	
			4" Battery fired 25 rounds. 3" " " 9 " OJ 10c in a conference of OC Bde 'A' & 'B' with Gen Robinson, 0.B. & Brig Major was held at 2nd Bde. NQTA discuss artillery action, withdrawing from firing line in event of enemy's advance. Gun as to where fire can be opened from NO 1 Battery when gun is to check fire	
	28/4/15			

WAR DIARY or INTELLIGENCE SUMMARY

Army Form C. 2118

4th NORTHUMBRIAN HOW. BDE. R.F.A.

Place	Date	Hour	Summary of Events and Information	Remarks and references to Appendices
	27/4/15		4" Battery fired 26 rounds 5" " " 17 " O.C. Bde & O.C's batteries at H.Q. had a conference on joint cycle O.P. &c.	
	28/4/15		4" Battery fired 26 rounds 5" " " nil " Clear day. Some fairly heavy shelling particularly 4 guns in afternoon 4" Battery two rounds of gunfire into position 12 m N (?) of 5 reg'tl gutter with 4.0 m added 5" Battery during night fired in addition over trench 40. O.C. Bde visited 150 & 54 Bdes 4" Battery fired 6 rounds 5" " " 30 rounds	
	29/4/15		In afternoon 1", 2", & 4" of 4" batt'n Bde carried by 47 & 49 1st Sgts 31". Had a combined shoot at 1 siegemin trench behind 40. The 18 Pdr & 3" How shooting were reported as good. The 5" How as inaccurate. Later in afternoon and evening a good deal of artillery activity. In vicinity of 50 Bn R.+ Bde H.Q. and road at H25 & 7.0 shelled & sniped intermittently Some 6 members of Col Dugs [?] had wound H24 & 9.0 east of Fredericsteen H.Q. Includes were killed on horseback 2 Col Horse of hounds 4 Smith were wounded & 6 killed. Ammunition as Committee B of R6 going with Corner as 5"How Battery took over to 5" Battery meeting ad.	

Army Form C. 2118

4th NORTHUMBRIAN HOW. BDE. R.F.A.

WAR DIARY
or
INTELLIGENCE SUMMARY
(Erase heading not required.)

Instructions regarding War Diaries and Intelligence Summaries are contained in F. S. Regs., Part II. and the Staff Manual respectively. Title Pages will be prepared in manuscript.

Place	Date	Hour	Summary of Events and Information	Remarks and references to Appendices
	30/12/15		4th Battery fired 30 rounds (17 + 13 HE) (13 30 P.M.) 5th " " 1 " (50 P.M.) Considerable shelling of roads by enemy, particularly in the evening when about 200 rounds H.E. were fired at & near Blauwepoorl — There were a little to S. of Anglican	
	31/12/15		6 4th Battery fired 161 rounds 5 " " 37 " (at 30 P.M.) 3 " " 37 " At 9.15 am the division on our right had a combined shot on enemy's front line trenches. The command a good deal of retaliation was shown. Stations of Dickebusch & Vlamertinghe shelled & enemy at available 5.9" gun firing from some point in the distance at 11 P.M. fired 5 rounds. Fire was objected at 12 m & in the whole of evening of trenches. Fire was again opened on trenches 12 A.M. 13th Div. front.	
	1/1/16		[illegible lines struck through]	

on Jan 1916

A.H. [signature] Lieut. Col. R.A.
Commdg. 4th North'n How. Bde. R.F.A. (T.F.)

50

1/4 North br Bde
R F A

Jan & Feb
Vol. VIII

4th NORTHUMBRIAN HOW. BDE. R.F.A.

WAR DIARY or INTELLIGENCE SUMMARY

Army Form C. 2118

Place	Date	Hour	Summary of Events and Information	Remarks and references to Appendices
	1/4/16		4" Battery fired 17 2ary 3 3 L/I = 350 Rounds	
			5" " 11 " " " = 15 - 5" -	
			O/C Bde. and Adjt. looking for Gun positions & over 3 H.Q 2	
			A & 2 Bdes. were placed in positions in rear of H.Q XIII	
	2/4/16		4" Battery fired nil rounds	
			5" " " 3 hay	
			A ass and dep. Little artillery activity	
			O/C 4" Battery & Adjt. examined Gun positions for 2 H.Q 2	
	3/4/16		4" Battery fired 31 Lg.H = 31 rounds	
			5" " " 1 " — 16 hay = 16 - 1 —	
			A Hostile activity by 11 cms howitzer. considerable artillery activity	
			on both sides	
			Commanding & O.C. B Co. carried out a tactics round K.H. 60 hot.	
			Nord. K. 10 2 and 4 of John steam Bn. & 47 Inf. Big. Hd.	
			Ind. 5" Battery saw nos 147 (O.P.)	
	4/4/16		4" Battery fired 18 hang = 23 L.g.H = 41 Rounds	
			5" " " " 71 Hay	
			Dull day O/C Bde & Adjt. went to "Bullford" & saw No 2 new Emplacements completed	

Army Form C. 2118

WAR DIARY or INTELLIGENCE SUMMARY

(Erase heading not required.)

4th Northumbrian How. Bde. R.F.A.

Place	Date	Hour	Summary of Events and Information	Remarks and references to Appendices
	5/4/16		Clear day and a good deal of Artillery activity. 5th Durham Battery fired 100 rounds teargas at W.M.80 in response to a request from 6th N.F. who were being shelled. Enemy shelling was replied to by the infantry & enemy fire was silenced. 4th Durham Battery fired 25 rounds at Clonard Copse by request of 3rd Bde. Close 3rd Battery were trying shells and fire was silenced. No district around Bryère Hurricaine was later shelled in W.P. feature.	
	6/4/16		Dull day & fairly quiet. Both batteries fired at the request of infantry about 1 p.m. damage 50 how + 8 light = 58 [most for retaliation or 4th Battery fired 50 how + 8 light = 58] 5" 1 " " 122 " 122 4th Battery fired 45 how + 25 light = 70 S " 21 " " 21 " About day + w/o Cpt Kennyon Artillery on patrol the entire 4th Battery front arrived at Bichtpearn	

46th NORTHUMBRIAN HOW. BDE. R.F.A.

WAR DIARY or **INTELLIGENCE SUMMARY**

Army Form C. 2118

Place	Date	Hour	Summary of Events and Information	Remarks and references to Appendices
	6/7/16		Both batteries took part in a small barrage scheme arranged by CRA; 5th Battery fired 40 rounds at 2 p.m. & 4th Battery the same amount at 2.30 p.m. During the latter scheme the infantry reported that a front store was blown up by one of our rounds at U.19.60.7. At 2.30 p.m. the 5th Battery were shelled and one of their emplacements was hit with the result that the ammunition pit was set on fire & 114 cartridges (50 pdr) were burnt. He fire wasted out but not before some wheels and harness were complete ?? One gun wheel was slightly burnt + the dial sight broken. At 2.50 p.m. 3rd Bde reported that their batteries at Blauwepoort were being shelled + asked us to retaliate. The 4th Battery was ordered to fire 100 rounds at Clonmel Copse and the enemy shelling ceased. Our fire did much damage to dug-outs in front trenches and other points engaged.	
	9/7/16		A pre-arranged bombardment of Hill 60 by heavy artillery and our divisional artillery took place between 11 a.m. & 1 p.m. The 5th Battery took part and fired 160 rounds (50 pdr). The 4th Battery stood by in case of enemy retaliation but was not called upon as the retaliation was very slight on their Zone.	

Army Form C. 2118

4th NORTHUMBRIAN HOW. BDE. R.F.A.

WAR DIARY or INTELLIGENCE SUMMARY
(Erase heading not required.)

Instructions regarding War Diaries and Intelligence Summaries are contained in F.S. Regs., Part II. and the Staff Manual respectively. Title Pages will be prepared in manuscript.

Place	Date	Hour	Summary of Events and Information	Remarks and references to Appendices
[illegible]	10/1/16		At noon whilst going to the acceptance of a wounded [gunner?] the 3rd Bde [Bgde] who was hit while pushing down to the 5th Battery Major F. W. PAYNTER was struck by a piece of an killed instantly. Lieut. Salbury + some other NCOs were also on the spot. Death almost instantaneous. Patrol was the on the one hit. He was buried near Railway Dugouts at 9 pm. W. P. G. Pl. pl. presented, Capt Ainsley [?] & Lt Ainslie Scarr Chatterton + OC 3rd Bde RFA — [Col] [illegible] was present. OC Brigade from OC 3rd Bde RFA — [Cap] Williams + Lieut Maples + Major Payne [?] [illegible] Auth [?] Battery Sgt Maj [illegible] [illegible] sent as gathering some mementoes to the correspondence of the deceased Major. Nos contents of the [illegible] was entirely respected. No contents of the [illegible] ammunition. That so far as can be stated has been his life sent to any [illegible] ordered in Armentières. [illegible] 12 more 3 lb to 75 battery which is [illegible] and SOS [illegible] [illegible] 60 rounds were fired today [illegible] [illegible] 5th Battery fund is now bringing up del.	

Army Form C. 2118

4th NORTHUMBRIAN HOW. BDE. R.F.A.

WAR DIARY
or
INTELLIGENCE SUMMARY
(Erase heading not required.)

Instructions regarding War Diaries and Intelligence Summaries are contained in F. S. Regs., Part II. and the Staff Manual respectively. Title Pages will be prepared in manuscript.

Place	Date	Hour	Summary of Events and Information	Remarks and references to Appendices
	11/4/16		Quiet day on the whole. Both batteries fired a few rounds of night fire. 3/5" Battery commenced ranging in the afternoon.	
	12/4/16		Registered up till 10.30 a.m. after which the weather was too hazy for observation. Batteries fired for 2 hours in the afternoon at trenches & strong points. 2/5" fired 50/A on shelters & 3/B Battery [illegible]	
	13/4/16		Fairly quiet day & too windy for aeroplane observation. 5" Battery disturbed in the afternoon at the request of infantry.	
	14/4/16		Fairly quiet day. 1st, 2nd and 3rd R.B. fired on enemy trenches. 3rd finished (3 [illegible] used to make [illegible]) and in the afternoon. fired [illegible] [illegible] Enemy replied on French & 3rd don't [illegible] [illegible] trenches with shrapnel 3" 5" Battery watched and any enemy [illegible] fired [illegible] Capt Brown returned to Ammn Col.	

4th NORTHUMBRIAN HOW. BDE. R.F.A.

WAR DIARY or INTELLIGENCE SUMMARY

Army Form C. 2118

Place	Date	Hour	Summary of Events and Information	Remarks and references to Appendices
	15/1/16		Quiet morning. In afternoon a considerable amount of enemy shelling round Potijze and by our Chateau. Our 1 Gun Battery Howitzer in H15d came into action. Enemy fire appears broken [up?] & Battery zone'd for.	
	16/1/16		A quiet day. 4th Battery fired on J19a5f and landed round 7 to 20 yards on either side of aiming point.	
	17/1/16		A very fine clear morning. Quite aerial activity. An immense bombardment of enemy just East & South of Potijze and work was carried out by 15 Pdr, 5" How, 6" How & 9.2 How. A great deal of damage was done to enemy trench. Our 1 Gun Aeroplane was trumped down at Potijze. No lost very appreciable. The enemy shelled heavily on our trenches with "whizz bangs" 4.2's & 5.9's doing considerable damage but no casualties (infantry) were reported. 15 Pdr Battery Co[r]p[o]r[a]l Walsted and from 2 h 3.45 had a Hate Member of 4.2 was falling - no damage. O/C Batty visit communication work Gen. [Cook?] of Heads and had a narrow escape. Adjut[ant] went through no barrage — no casualties.	

1875 Wt. W593/826 1,000,000 4/15 J.B.C. & A. A.D.S.S./Forms/C. 2118.

4th NORTHUMBRIAN HOW. BDE. R.F.A.

WAR DIARY or INTELLIGENCE SUMMARY

Army Form C. 2118

Place	Date	Hour	Summary of Events and Information	Remarks and references to Appendices
Ypres	13/7/15		A dull day. Late turning to heavy rain. Little artillery activity on either side, for a few minutes 5" Battery watched about 8 enemy shells to hobs over dutch of CRA O.C. Bde 1 Lft to hobs over dutch of Major R Chapman DSO who was dutch of O/C Bde. on leave. Nine were later seen by Brigade on ashore. 8 huns + 5 News were later seen by Brigade on ashore.	
	14/7/15		A light clear day. OA 9.15 enemy commenced what was evidently an offensive bombardment of our front line trenches. Retaliation was ordered by both howitzer + [...] and 11" R 96 - 41° Left Bn. [...] C.11.6.a. On continuance to observe for 4" Battery on hostile fire could not be opened owing to our own howitzer + [...] covering [...] 2nd Bn. 123 Bde was ordered to support infantry, and added [...] of considerable fire burst 101 5.9 when Germans [...] front. NP W.W was under our fire to day, I have kept adopted great [...] of a Battery position was nearby Wood + Rifflers was broken.	

4th NORTHUMBRIAN HOW. BDE. R.F.A.

WAR DIARY or INTELLIGENCE SUMMARY

Army Form C. 2118

Place	Date	Hour	Summary of Events and Information	Remarks and references to Appendices
Ypres	20/9/15		A dull quiet day. O/C Bde & O/C 5th Battery selected new positions for 2 guns of 5th Bty.	
	21/9/15		A dull day. Little artillery activity.	
	22/9/15		A clear morning. Carefully taken O/C Bde O/C 5th Bty & Adjutant spent morning watching forward positions also inspected new emplacements for 2 guns in Chicory Patch. Enemy shelled 4th & 5th Battery. About 3 p.m. 4th Battery was heavily shelled about 100 S.E. was clearly seen. The 5th section No Casualties. 5th June. The greater number of shells fell round 4 left section in support of the infantry and managed to help up fire with No 1 gun. No other Exp. Tel. Line communication with trenches & N P. Later all wires were cut & to with the of Staff Ing (Wilson) & 5th Bde made a wind to the right of the Battery.	

4th NORTHUMBRIAN HOW. BDE. R.F.A.

WAR DIARY or INTELLIGENCE SUMMARY

Army Form C. 2118

Place	Date	Hour	Summary of Events and Information	Remarks and references to Appendices
			The F.S.O. 24th Division who was passing was complimented the O/c Battery & B.S.M. on their devotion to duty and also wrote C.R.A. 50th Division O/c Bde received the following from C.R.A. 50th Div. "Will you please convey to Capt. Chapman the B.S.M. & 2 Bombardiers of 4th Durham Battery my appreciation of their cool & gallant conduct on the afternoon of 22nd Jan. in maintaining the fire of this Battery in support of our infantry when the telephone station was a hunter way shell fire. I should like their names noted for mention in dispatches in connection with this & a note made in diary."	B.S.M. Sergt. Wilson ...
	23/1/16		A dark misty morning. Clearing later. A particularly clear forenoon with numerous aircraft about, shortly afterwards all followed & H.Q.'s were very nebulous enemy planes being up nearly all day. In afternoon O/c Bde (Maj Chapman DSO) & Adjt visited 4 Battery & inspected work of shelling in previous day. It was considered best to leave same in meantime.	

WAR DIARY or INTELLIGENCE SUMMARY

Army Form C. 2118

4th Northumbrian How. Bde. R.F.A.

Place	Date	Hour	Summary of Events and Information	Remarks and references to Appendices
	24/1/16		A dull morning. Bright later. Little artillery activity. In afternoon enemy shelled neighbourhood of 3rd Durham Battery front. Commenced at about 3.20 P.M. with 15·9 line HE bursting very high. Interval between rounds was 3 to 5 minutes. Fire 2 round salvos. Fire ceased at 4.45. Our total salvos 77 rounds. No damage or casualties. Fire was in constance up to 6 of the shots on ornaments was burst behind No. 6's gun. One of the one's went to No. 1. 2 & 3. 7. 8. Bonny of IA8 shells fell near 5th Durham Battery but there were no casualties. Coff Primo came to H.Q. to stay over night. 2 Enfield took our own Open art.	
	25/1/16		A fairly clear day. Bad aeroplane activity. Enemy planes were flying over both batteries nearly all day and our anti aircraft gun + ammo was unable to keep them in check. Our army was frequently shelled. Enemy planes were also continually behind Ypres and Sanders read. Capt Bruno took over Command of 5th Battery. S. Yolland (5th Battery) was injured in Ackagh Wood. His working stick was struck by a bullet	

Army Form C. 2118

4th NORTHUMBRIAN HOW. BDE. R.F.A.

WAR DIARY
or
INTELLIGENCE SUMMARY
(Erase heading not required.)

Instructions regarding War Diaries and Intelligence Summaries are contained in F. S. Regs., Part II. and the Staff Manual respectively. Title Pages will be prepared in manuscript.

Place	Date	Hour	Summary of Events and Information	Remarks and references to Appendices
	26/1/16		A dull damp morning. O/c Bde & Adjt spent morning selecting reserve gun positions for C. in O₂. Capt. Prime & Capt. Anderson (5" Battery) went to trenches to reconnoitre a dug-out, while they were away 8 shell (4" & shrapnel & percussion) were fired round French Farm one bursting on top. 8 Officers killed – 20 casualties. Major Chapman D.S.O. walked out to 4" Battery which he was there the battery was heavily shelled he carried on all his men quickly cleared to shelter some distance away. 2 dug-outs were totally damaged but is from men his Major Bronfman D.S.O. & Offr. Jos. Dumas was watching for an Observation battery who were aiming down these trenches was in good humour	
	27/1/16		A dull day. 13th Artillery Column. In morning 5" Battery fired on Weltje on kill 60. Col. Stoelky returned from 30th R.A.	

1875 Wt. W593/826 1,000,000 4/15 J.B.C. & A. A.D.S.S./Forms/C. 2118.

WAR DIARY or INTELLIGENCE SUMMARY

Army Form C. 2118

4th NORTHUMBRIAN HOW. BDE. R.F.A.

Place	Date	Hour	Summary of Events and Information	Remarks and references to Appendices
	29/1/16		O/c Bde & Adjt. of 5" Battery, 151st Ay Bde H.Q.'s. A dull morning. Was Artillery Activity. Windsor all moved to 3rd Bde. H.Q.s	
	30/1/16		O/c Bde & Adjt. of 6" Battery afterwards O/c Bde with Capt. Ivin Paterson Brinson went to tatting & inspected all dumps.	
			A dull quiet day. Very muddy & cold. Both Brigades went to 2nd R.A. in cars for C.H.Q.	
	31/1/16		A dull quiet day. Some shelling of trenches. Batteries of Brigade were included in new trenches system from 6 P.M.	
			5/6.	

AMPocken Lieut. Col. R.A.
Commdg. 4th North'n How. Bde. R.F.A. (T.F.)

Army Form C. 2118

4th Northumbrian How. Bde. R.F.A.

WAR DIARY
or
INTELLIGENCE SUMMARY
(Erase heading not required.)

Instructions regarding War Diaries and Intelligence Summaries are contained in F. S. Regs, Part II. and the Staff Manual respectively. Title Pages will be prepared in manuscript.

Place	Date	Hour	Summary of Events and Information	Remarks and references to Appendices

Brigade Officers on him have known list

Attached on Infantry

Lt Col. A. W. Hoathly R.A.
Major R. Stokman
2/Capt. S.K. Anderson
2/Capt. C. J. Stokman
Lt. W. Yielding
Lt. J. he Dan
B. W. B. Carnell (Killed in Action July 10th 1915)

D.S.O — Major R. Stokman
Military Cross — Lt. J. L. Stokman
D.C.M. — L. J. Lambrooks

50

1/4 Nbrm Bde R.F.a.

Vol IX

Army Form C. 2118

4th NORTHUMBRIAN HOW. BDE. R.F.A.

WAR DIARY
or
INTELLIGENCE SUMMARY
(Erase heading not required.)

Instructions regarding War Diaries and Intelligence Summaries are contained in F. S. Regs., Part II. and the Staff Manual respectively. Title Pages will be prepared in manuscript.

Place	Date	Hour	Summary of Events and Information	Remarks and references to Appendices
	1/7/16		Dull morning. Heavy rain from account of artillery activity on British front line & back line. Our batteries and line answered by heavy. Little response on future and to enemy.	
	2/7/16		Dull morning. Fired 54 Rifles later. A quiet day C.Os visited front line and began to Colonel 150 Inf. Bde Command.	
	3/7/16		A quiet day. Weather wind and dry. Hundreds aeroplane activity.	
	4/7/16		A fairly quiet day but some trench mortars. Reply to Obrecourt. A good day in week with artillery. Gun fire was heavy and rather slack of evening. In enemy considerable enemy shelling on veneer front. Not much done.	
	5/7/16		A very quiet day. But some trench activity. Counter battery some machine gun. Some counter on horizon follows. Fair amount of artillery activity on with sides.	

1875 Wt. W593/826 1,000,000 4/15 J.B.C. & A. A.D.S.S./Forms/C. 2118.

WAR DIARY
or
INTELLIGENCE SUMMARY

Army Form C. 2118

4th NORTHUMBRIAN HOW. BDE. R.F.A.

Place	Date	Hour	Summary of Events and Information	Remarks and references to Appendices
	6/2/16		A fairly clear day both batteries fired a good deal in early morning. In early afternoon heavy enemy shelling behind the line particularly round Hulluloval. About 100 enemy Command shelling round 2 rear guns of 5th Battery. 90 rounds of 4.2" & 5.9" were put in (25 Hows.) One unexploded was dil but the gun was but damaged. There were no casualties. Heavy hv. wbos of french fell near our guns. 8:30 pm firing commenced & detachments were closed	
	7/2/16		A very clear day, with the result that very considerable activity by aeroplanes and artillery was experienced. The 4th Battery was shelled and a few shells were again dropped on the 2 rear guns of the 5th Battery. 2nd Lieut. M'G. McCallum returned for duty & was posted to the 5th Battery. 2nd Lieut. J.G. Pence also joined for duty & was attacked to the 4th Battery. The relief of one 5" gun by a 4.5" gun was safely accomplished by each battery.	
	8/2/16		Another very clear day rendering artillery difficult for our guns to fire much enemy to the continual activity of German aeroplanes. There was considerable enemy artillery activity all day The 4th Battery was shelled in the morning again at 6-7:30 pm, 8-4:5 pm, & 11-1:15 pm but there were no casualties & no damage with the exception of one hit on a dug-out. The 5th Battery were also shelled in	

WAR DIARY or INTELLIGENCE SUMMARY

Army Form C. 2118

4th NORTHUMBRIAN HOW. BDE. R.F.A.

Place	Date	Hour	Summary of Events and Information	Remarks and references to Appendices
	8/2/16		the morning, whilst at night, from 7 – 7.30, the roads & tracks around trench house received upwards of 100 shells, 6 of which were on the billet. The ration cart was there at the time the team stampeded, but were subsequently recovered and little damage was found to have been done. Lieut. W. Golding was slightly wounded by a piece of shell on the cheek & has gone to hospital. There were no other casualties. Both batteries registered with the 4.5 gun. 2nd Lieut. J.W. Dopwath + 2nd Lieut. J. L. Gilson, 3/4th Northumbrian (How) Bde joined for 14 days instruction and were attached to the 4th + 5th Batteries respectively.	
	9/2/16		Another very bright & clear day. Enemy aeroplane & artillery activity were very noticeable, the latter very much hampering the fire of our batteries. There was a certain amount of enemy fire in the early morning. The 4th Battery reporting shelling at 2.15 am & 4 am. During this the previous two days three enemy observation balloons were in evidence, they are put up for comparatively short period & then taken down but only to subsequently appear again. During the evening and night the enemy, as on the previous night, indulged in desultory shelling of the roads with 4.7 cm + 2" guns, this is believed to have relation to the relief being carried out on our right. The relief of a second 5" gun was safely accomplished by each battery.	
	10/2/16		A quiet day, cloudy but fine. Owing to weather conditions not being favourable no annoyance by aeroplanes was experienced. There was also a marked diminution in enemy shelling. Both batteries continued to register the 4.5 guns. After darkness fell the enemy again commenced dropping shells here & there in a desultory manner along the roads & continued the practice at intervals for some hours	

WAR DIARY or INTELLIGENCE SUMMARY

4th Northumbrian How. Bde. R.F.A.

Army Form C. 2118

Place	Date	Hour	Summary of Events and Information	Remarks and references to Appendices
	11/2/16		A cold, wet + very cloudy day. There was no aeroplane activity of any sort, but a good deal of artillery activity prevailed throughout the day. The 4th Battery were the recipients of 60 shells from about 7-45 am onwards. The evening + night were again marked by persistent shell-fire on our roads at frequent intervals. Col. Strachley returned from leave. The relief of the third gun was accomplished by each battery.	
	12/2/16		A cold + very cloudy day. The sky cleared for an hour or two in the middle of the day but again became obscured. No aeroplane activity of any sort was to be noted all day. There was, however, no slackening of artillery fire. About 2 P.M. a May Limp (searchlight?) type mine took place on an LG1 that was seen about a few rounds of enemy activity on enemy post. Enemy first battered LG1 about 6.30 PM and this to fire responded on 30 + rounds post. Enemy post was again heavily battered subsequently by LG1 between 9 & 11 Pot with shots shrapnel. In Our Fire Trench of Pilgrim Trench here was this considerable delay throughout about by Pilgrim Trench itself	
	13/2/16		Enemy very heavy trench mortar on woods was very heavy from 10 to 11 guns it was very quiet until dusk. John in the very quiet and there was a few a good class of enemy shelling all round with 4.2 Pilgrim Bulloc & faun Farm in for a good deal of dusting mostly by while there were out some 2 P.M. a 4.5 How scored a direct hit by casualties	
			There is a considerable enemy shelling in woods all night	

WAR DIARY or INTELLIGENCE SUMMARY

Army Form C. 2118

4th Northumbrian How. Bde. R.F.A.

(Erase heading not required.)

Instructions regarding War Diaries and Intelligence Summaries are contained in F.S. Regs., Part II. and the Staff Manual respectively. Title Pages will be prepared in manuscript.

Place	Date	Hour	Summary of Events and Information	Remarks and references to Appendices
	17/4/15		A weakly [?] about 11am O.C. P.H.s O. of 4th Battery trying for an observation [?]. A fairly brisk morning though enemy scattered shells all round. At 12h afternoon enemy opened a heavy bombardment on Division on our right of 1st Battery assisted in retaliation. At 1st [?] were being [?] shelled Division on our left very heavily. Battery assisted in retaliation. Fire of How. was not heavily [?]. An attack upon enemy trenches on our [?] A3, +4 & 5th we [?] trenches [?]. At 1800 trenches driven back by our barrage. An attack on our 11 Division developed & enemy making a further attack and [?] succeeded. At 3:30 [?] a number of [?], there [?] our [?] A counter attack was launched at 4:30 & at 5.00 Gd known of enemy being in [?] was able to be [?] 5½ trenches. During afternoon & early evening enemy heavily shelled all round trenches [?] from trenches. Gd trenches at times were full of [?] gas & [?] shells were sent up. During the day at 7:30 [?] to [?] posted C.R.E. (S.P.) which enabled him to call [?] for a short while. At 8pm our [?] [?] gas jets. It was decided to [?] report [?] [?]	

Army Form C. 2118

4th NORTHUMBRIAN HOW. BDE. R.F.A.

WAR DIARY or INTELLIGENCE SUMMARY

(Erase heading not required.)

Place	Date	Hour	Summary of Events and Information	Remarks and references to Appendices
	15/4/16		O.C. Bde took up his residence with left gp group Comdr. at Reninghelst. Adjt + remainder of H.Q. staff removed to H.Q. wagon lines. A fairly quiet day. At night our division rather heavy shelling a heavy bombardment took place on our right. A counter attack was launched but did not meet with total success. Lt Forsyth 4" Battery killed in trenches.	
	16/4/16		A very quiet day practically no artillery activity. Capt Cooper + Lt Wright wounded at 5" Battery Bn Dawson of Amm Col wounded near Trafael Corner delivering tombs.	
	17/4/16		A cold rather windy clear day. Division on our right (the ..?..) is not confirmed & . . . . . retained "The Bluff" which . . . . A quiet day on the whole.	
	18/4/16		Close to Bonn[?] Town near H.Q. bombed by enemy plane. A and attempted Adjt at wagn line a heavy bombardment of the Bluff by our heavy guns in evening. A quiet day on our front.	

A clear morning with some rain, OC 4" Battery & Adj't again looked
for an alternative position for 4" Battery. It was later decided by
CRA not to move and abandon the present position.
OC 5th RA &
In afternoon our Division left on the Bluff finding considerable substation
behind Hurreford and Colt. Balfe asked
CO Ordnan. & Adj't found 5" R Battery same position so that
considerable enemy shelling was but actually in 4" Battery

2/7/11
A fairly fine day. Enemy shelling in advance factory all day
our Batt. except Intermit. John D 61 Ryf. Woods shown (Dyff pack-)
fired the Brigade and fired two rounds to 5" R.Coy. major was
CO 5/6(?) but limited in attempts to Rgt Bomf Cmdr. and annoyed it worked
an extra and remained
On dinner a long talk followed by our Parties. The finished station partly
with 4" so still

2/7/11
A mild fairly warm with some rain. Little Artillery activity OC 61 at four
failed. In afternoon 4 Artillery again heavily shelled by a German S.g.
in order to little annoyed as and O Cres throughout a fair little also find
Inter Cochran O/J/1 joined 5 am
50th Divisional (late Battery) & Adjt arranged with L. Guy and B. Brown of 60th
Divisional for time in YPRES.

23/4/16 A cold morning with heavy cannonade during the day. H.Q. putting up a forward
O.P. H. Observing for Infantry and heavy. A few [?] from Bosch with which [?]
[?] German Staff. [?] [?] to him on Y.M.5. D.61 worked with supplementals.

24/4/16 O.C. who went out at 8 during battery's 2nd round met C/S. Osborne & Yates
wounded to H.Q. Sitting taken over on D.61 [?]. C out of action
[?] [?] [?] [?]. Under the Culture order by an S.H. shell
3.5. Dixon wounded at noon. Sie by putting out aid by shell (5.9 [?] on Battery)
a bit of snow. S.H. Battery had to retaliate.

25/4/16 A cold windy day. Sent fresh 13th division on Enemy Artillery especially put
heavy [?] hill 6 about 4 P.M. D/P. [?].
[?] O.P. by a sniper in dug-out. D.61 [?]. T.A. Dickey [?] and new machine.
a quiet day.

26/4/16 A bitterly cold morning. S.P. shell of some sort rather heavier amongst Cart Gands
a shower in late afternoon. A. [?] fall & [?] at H.Q.'s not [?] at L.G. at H.Q.
[?] [?] ordered to our 2nd forward [?]. B. half & pair of [?] Sitter.
[?] bombed our completed O.P. by 1.0 P.M.
O.C. O.B.C. & O/R. to inspect new Battery [?] and relieved [?] [?] S. D.61
D.61 [?] [?] on our [?] [?]
[?] of [?] Riding a shop Inf. Office [?] [?] from H.Q. for Relief on Bde. (5th Battery)
D [?] [?] Effer from pp for Bde. (5th Battery) a missing Guardsman

4th NORTHUMBRIAN HOW. BDE. R.F.A.

27/2/16 Otto more shiny the night a shew set in. A still day
         but little Ostling activity
         hostile hostility fired a round. Alfred J Brown always toward Indian confirmed

28/2/16 A brightish milder morning
         No artillery activity

29/2/16 A bright morning. Considerable enemy aeroplane activity
         Both hostiles had a quiet day
         In early afternoon enemy opened heavy fire on many heavy batteries
         & actions round Dichebush Huiseland wood and in neighbourhood of
         Huiseland. 4" Battery activity (2 Powell) while on road to H Q got a
         piece of shell in his leg. He was dressed & managed to join of shell
         Lt.? from P6. Bty was wounded in the arm by piece of shell
         5" Battery telephone communication to front had
         3° gunners (4 Battery) wounded at new gun position in YPRES. (in leg.)

                                                    [signature]
                                                    LIEUT. Col. R.A.
                                                    Commande. 4th. North'n How. Bde. R.F.A. (T.F.)

3/16
5/16

Army Form C. 2118.

4th NORTHUMBRIAN HOW. BDE. R.F.A.

WAR DIARY
or
INTELLIGENCE SUMMARY.
(Erase heading not required.)

Place	Date	Hour	Summary of Events and Information	Remarks and references to Appendices
	1/5/16		A dull morning which cleared later. Artillery quiet O/C Bde. Adjt. at Gunnery lectures at Poperinghe & after at Omer Bat. and Battery lines. At 5 P.M. an Artillery Bombardment of enemy trenches in Biff 'C' Wood opened on us in 14 & 15. The fire was continued with great intensity till 5.45 P.M. and then slowly till 6.45. In addition to the 12 Bde. S & 3" we had 60 Bd. 6" Gun , 6" How, 9.2" & 15" How on board. A heavy battle was then absolute control of the air obtained by our planes, we had about 14 up and not a single German seen. Also WEST OF YPRES. Guns were fired at from all parts of the Salient but as expected up the dugouts saved us light Other than this Night was quiet + 4.2 How on Bilhim + 5" battery fired on local spots. Lieut Enroll + L¹ Wilson & Sewell rejoined from Base	

WAR DIARY
or
INTELLIGENCE SUMMARY.
(Erase heading not required.)

Army Form C. 2118.

Place	Date	Hour	Summary of Events and Information	Remarks and references to Appendices
	2/3/16		At 4-30 am all our guns opened with a very heavy fire on enemy front line, trenches and strong points. Fire was answered & continued till 5-45 am. Guns had been with drills twice & again we fired all night. Enemy fire very heavy also in addition to the trenches on many batteries & other points round our line. During the day our planes were able to help enemy things to east of YPRES. Guns Nos 1,2,3, down enemy trenches near The Bluff. Nos 1, 2 in a Hog L(?) Hill & our wire still tracts. Guns 4,5,6, continued on The Bluff till 5-45 am. Heavy enemy shelling particularly time HE over our lines all along Bedchester ridge on to Rumilies(?) and over hour. Of our guns Shelma Tower was used to 4 Corps attack about noon. Bluff in event + of our Hill, The Bluff and all our op-less(?) had been wasted(?). All our Limits(?) to small ammunition had ten rifled along right + ammunition remained in good demand.	

WAR DIARY or INTELLIGENCE SUMMARY
Army Form C. 2118.

Place	Date	Hour	Summary of Events and Information	Remarks and references to Appendices
	4/7/16		Whole line on Beaumont at 4am.	

D.61. when full extent of work had magnitude of own shells to be seen — no casualties reported —

11.0pm – Enemy opened fire on 2 Officers & 150 other German prisoners filed onwards. A report taken 11.8 men on the whole.

1st Battery fired 215 rounds (Counter Battery) unobserved

by Milling of Milling HQ a considerable amount was
fired from Leon 15."0b Bulehole unsatisfactory as I went

2nd Gun Ground (am 100 yards) much too near our own trenches
On the White Pumps were quiet

3rd Battery fired 393 rounds on the 2 Inhabited Houses and fallen
in Wolfedere. Officers of R.G.A. Canada.
Lance Corporal D. B. Stooge with wounded & came into Battery in
about the latter sighting on by
f.O.C. B.330rnds white end Inach 15/Very Poor to Enemy not building.
If 2 on 6.9 Open In Observers and 3 man for 1/2 hour

WAR DIARY
or
INTELLIGENCE SUMMARY.
(Erase heading not required.)

Instructions regarding War Diaries and Intelligence Summaries are contained in F. S. Regs., Part II. and the Staff Manual respectively. Title pages will be prepared in manuscript.

Army Form C. 2118.

Place	Date	Hour	Summary of Events and Information	Remarks and references to Appendices
	2/3/16		Casualties [illegible] were caused by [illegible] shells over guns At 7 a.m. about 100 prisoners and a number of wounded Gordons came past battery. All spoken to both our men & prisoners said our Artillery work had been magnificent The prisoners were generally much shaken & some were wounded. They all seemed relieved to be out of the shell inferno" The Cycle orderly between Battery & HQ^s had a rough journey. As he crossed the canal the bridge he had just come over was blown up by an enemy shell. He had many times to take refuge in old dug outs & trenches but managed to get through Since the battery took over it has daily [illegible] " [illegible] for 10 weeks [illegible] [illegible] get through. Lt Smith had close shave being only a few yards off when 5.9^s burst [illegible]	

T2134. Wt. W708–776. 500000. 4/15. Sir J. C. & S.

WAR DIARY
or
INTELLIGENCE SUMMARY

(Erase heading not required.)

Army Form C. 2118.

Place	Date	Hour	Summary of Events and Information	Remarks and references to Appendices
	2/7/16		Sun of 100 6.1 C.H. and 300 5" guns used in total C.2 yrds casualties	
	3/7/16		6th Heavy Artillery Gp reply on 6", 8" & 9.2" Hs Brennan was quiet, Hostility by enemy artillery – Our own was especially with heavy trench mortar — Little activity — Of enemy trench guns to our batteries. Reports held that 1 another Gp of prisoners were taken to 1 Bn Gf and HQ at our trenches had been consolidated. Front line of enemy over Bois N.E. mary. night. Our guns rode into enemy and dealt by Lance Bn Major Guy Price, Lieut Park Lt & 2nd Gp guns swept during night Pad HQ to 4.14 by 3rd find cover away to highin stated Bath fullness road a further 100s about being the Gp1 from some 20yds West of Lyon .... DS.D. stood lores trace.	
	4/7/16		A Heavy inspection with a 6" Hwy society wind. Side of Artillery find to crush 4" Battery from 10 F. & 2nd howitzers with mor het vines in hilling with a few	

Instructions regarding War Diaries and Intelligence Summaries are contained in F. S. Regs., Part II. and the Staff Manual respectively. Title pages will be prepared in manuscript.

WAR DIARY
or
INTELLIGENCE SUMMARY.
(Erase heading not required.)

Army Form C. 2118.

Place	Date	Hour	Summary of Events and Information	Remarks and references to Appendices
	4/3/16		5th Battery lost a few 4.2 hows but not in Gallery. Reinhart was heavily shelled and L group HQs (2nd Bde.) was badly knocked about by about 60 5.9s. A move was made to opposite side of road. Instructions received that after all Division was not to be relieved [illegible] and that we (4th Bde.) were to take over R group on 8th inst. [illegible] that [illegible] were again [illegible] attacking Verdun. Lt. Weddell [illegible] with influenza. [illegible] in day & D61 section was left practically under water.	
	5/3/16		A bright cold morning with snow clouds at intervals. Enemy Planes did a fair amount of [illegible] near Dickebush & Crendon Hut. Also near H.Q. [illegible] (12th [illegible]) [illegible] for instruction to 35th Div. 4th Battery had heavy enemy shelling [illegible] and [illegible] a [illegible]. [illegible]. 5th Battery had a quiet day.	

T2134. Wt. W708–776. 500000. 4/15. Sir J. C. & S.

WAR DIARY
or
INTELLIGENCE SUMMARY.
(Erase heading not required.)

Army Form C. 2118.

Place	Date	Hour	Summary of Events and Information	Remarks and references to Appendices
	30/3/16		A windy morning not a considerable quantity of snow which cleared with present sun. Our very own guns did well. O/C 106th + 105th at intervals in the (8" + 9.2 Howitzers) reported enemy front trenches on I obvious + opposite I, A Division a considerable bulge on the left of S.T. Sire. Some fire was also opened on the enemy lines by A Batteries + Co.s. 17th Division distant about 1/3'. Trench O.P. on a both west [?] right of homestead + Richebourg Junction came that enemy had commenced a counter offensive. 4" Battery fired a salvo on Chemint Capes + a few [?] of howitzer 5" Battery did not fire - too back[?] shelling.	
	31/3/16		A windy morning, snow showers which continued all day. A very good light practically no hostile by other side. O/C the Battalion O.P. found + H.Q. did not appear to be occupied to observed in Richebourg Village. The enemy sept[?] shell [?] on Richebourg L'Avoue in R.F.A. lines. [?] Followed by retaliation in our lines. Considerable shelling on neighborhood of car. I attack from No. 60 + No. 69 Battery	

WAR DIARY
or
INTELLIGENCE SUMMARY.
(Erase heading not required.)

Army Form C. 2118.

Place	Date	Hour	Summary of Events and Information	Remarks and references to Appendices
	9/9/16		A fairly passing out much sniper attly firing. When very slow with a number of burts about Op. 8 was area. 8101 J.m. or on on hill 9, a Forben and Lewis Which our own and Lewis scoreths being fired. The Forben kept firing the seam bursts fired at by our infantry and fell in German trench. What seems S.P. Battery wished orders to fire at various wheels outworthy to 2H houses on a suspected M.G. next to SP. Battery. Corpused firing on ho108 3 & Div. Battle valley on Col Pipe in enemy artillery. Bid but outburst 2 H LIV. 6 H HLI but outpour of S.BC's at Spot No.5. S.P. Battery noticed whils on march about. A quiet day on the whole. A damp dull morning. No artillery activity. S H BM. Continued to fire on Caithness wood left slightly slow rate. Opened 4 P.M. enemy observed to shell valley from M.2 & S.P. are trenches 3.7/1. etc This ordered 5.P.I. early 6 P.M. Suddenly our outward night on valley to our continual artillery.	

WAR DIARY
or
INTELLIGENCE SUMMARY.
(Erase heading not required.)

Army Form C. 2118.

Place	Date	Hour	Summary of Events and Information	Remarks and references to Appendices
	11/4/16		2nd Lt. Buford came to duty at 11.P. for instructional purposes.	
	12/4/16		A slight shelling with considerable aeroplane activity. We shelled our troops and enemy was quiet also. There were a few rounds of artillery fire exchanged. There was considerable activity unless by Minchin & Lieut Little Crooks.	
	13/4/16		A.M. Morning with considerable artillery activity. P.M. Remained quiet and so did the enemy. In afternoon there was heavy shelling behind the line by ourselves and considerable activity on the P.M.	
	14/4/16		Another light morning with considerable aeroplane activity. We again received quite to others quiet on open of trenches. Enemy slight twenty as and about finished and infantry unit was on D.O's.	
	15/4/16		A dull quiet morning but the enemy and A considerable artillery activity. In afternoon very many shelling of tops and later on our right but quiet on our actual front. Heavy many shelling around Wulverhem and M.O.'s a short future. Enemy using shells.	

WAR DIARY
or
INTELLIGENCE SUMMARY.
(Erase heading not required.)

Army Form C. 2118.

Place	Date	Hour	Summary of Events and Information	Remarks and references to Appendices
	14/1/17		A bright morning. Aircraft continue active. S.O.S. from T.M.B. & Army HQ. no reply on the	
			enemy. Our Batts. wires & Tel. Lines full on in	
			the front. N.R. & Mortars vigorously engaged	
			R.F.a. in 2 Belgian trenches to be checked by our guns	
			was arranged.	
			5" Battery did a little shooting.	
	15/1/17		A dull day. Enemy did a considerable amount of sniping	
			but our own was a little to. On 2 of the batteries (I forget	
			which) he ranged. 3" Battery identify were heavily shelled by counter	
			Our R.F.a. batteries were much too quiet. However we	
			did very much anything with our batteries	
			a little very slow fire at our batteries	
			had very slow. Enemy snipers ranging vigorously all round the salient	
			our Batteries did nothing to retaliate in form. We took down everything of	
			2 Heavy Bttys. 1 R.F.a. & 3" Battery & snipers N.C. H.R. killed	

Instructions regarding War Diaries and Intelligence Summaries are contained in F. S. Regs., Part II. and the Staff Manual respectively. Title pages will be prepared in manuscript.

WAR DIARY
or
INTELLIGENCE SUMMARY.
(*Erase heading not required.*)

Army Form C. 2118.

Place	Date	Hour	Summary of Events and Information	Remarks and references to Appendices
	19/3/16		Enemy aeroplanes kept our batteries quiet all day - an enemy did a considerable amount of shooting	
			5th Battery fired during the night at enemy work near [illegible] Cutting	
	20/3/16		Another fine day for enemy planes. Our batteries could do practically no shooting	
			5th Battery did practically no shooting	
	21/3/16		A dull day quiet on both sides	
			5th Battery assisted in small Counter battery actions. 1 Sec of 4th Bty	[illegible] over
	22/3/16		Another dull quiet day with a slight strafe commenced by the Hun in afternoon. Major Cochrane D.S.O took over 5th Battery from Major Dixon & section of 4th Battery completed the relief	
	[illegible]		A fairly quiet day with a small strafe in afternoon on our right	
			4th Battery [illegible] lines of fire 149th and 150th Bdes	(Inf)
	24/3/16		Heavy snowstorm. A quiet day. A great deal of [illegible] & [illegible]. 4th Battery registered	

T2134. Wt. W708–776. 500000. 4/15. Sir J. C. & S.

WAR DIARY
or
INTELLIGENCE SUMMARY.
(Erase heading not required.)

Army Form C. 2118.

Instructions regarding War Diaries and Intelligence Summaries are contained in F. S. Regs., Part II. and the Staff Manual respectively. Title pages will be prepared in manuscript.

Place	Date	Hour	Summary of Events and Information	Remarks and references to Appendices
	25/9/16		A bright morning with low clouds. A little aeroplane activity. Very little artillery activity of Infantry. Boche was seen about today mostly all afternoon. A little damage to entanglements on crossroads.	
	26/9/16		A wet morning with later a little snow. A little artillery activity in afternoon. On the whole a quiet day. Few many snow clouds for aeroplanes.	
	27/9/16		At 12.15 a.m. British on our right made an attack on 27 Divn trenches after putting up 6 minute rifle fire of objective but not the left. About 130 prisoners should up at 2 P.M. At 1.15" a counter attack was launched but NOH did not come to trenches. Afterwards our heavies continued counter battery work. & the enemy replied at night. Considerable shelling of YPRES, KRUISSTRAAT & district. A heavy bombardment of fight. 9/10 of objective attained.	

WAR DIARY
or
INTELLIGENCE SUMMARY.
(Erase heading not required.)

Army Form C. 2118.

Place	Date	Hour	Summary of Events and Information	Remarks and references to Appendices
	28/2/16		A dullish day. Fairly quiet on whole. No aeroplane activity. 4" Battery did a small concentration shoot. About 5 P.M. wind was strong & Whizbee N Whinchard was fairly shelled and two put over which was short & hit about 5.15 P.M.	
	29/2/16		A dullish day. Most frequent a live guns on different jobs. Enemy did very little and activity. So far as I know. 1 & 2 BCs Whizby Corner and rifle grenades from BCs Whizby Corner still.	
	1/3/16		A bright day. Considerable aeroplane activity and consequent heavy shelling in most parts of salient particularly Ypres Rd & Wieltzhoek district also round Square Wood. 4 Battery had a quiet day. 1st Div Canadian Artillery RCs came up to Kathinis	
	3/3/16		A bright but rather misty morning. No hours lost concerned and this was the enemy artillery activity. 4" Battery had a quiet day.	

W Hockley Lieut. Col. R.A.
Commdg. 4th North'n How. Bde. R.F.A. (T.F.)

50

1/4 N'rn Bde R.F.A

Vol X

Army Form C. 2118.

4th NORTHUMBRIAN HOW. BDE. R.F.A.

WAR DIARY
or
INTELLIGENCE SUMMARY.
(Erase heading not required.)

Instructions regarding War Diaries and Intelligence Summaries are contained in F. S. Regs., Part II. and the Staff Manual respectively. Title pages will be prepared in manuscript.

Place	Date	Hour	Summary of Events and Information	Remarks and references to Appendices
	1/4/16		Enemy firing on St Eloi during night, a hostile attack having been made, knowing light + fine. Our planes active. Rifle down enemy plane.	
	2/4/16		On a visit today went by left side with Major Pink. G/3 & Centre Battery went sharply in position. Enemy shelling of our trenches.	
	3/4/16		A lot of enemy, Corps Comd Brig Commander comes to take over in evening. 6 Hunters + Gen Staff Commander.	
			Stops on St Eloi continued further progress on our Right. Very heavy shelling all round back. Instructions went to N.C. (3rd Northumberland Bty) + Adjt (N.O.) slightly wounded.	
	4/4/16		Enemy firing all round N.O. during night. Lieut Chapman slightly also on N.O.S. Northern Officers building from the North. ½ relief completed at 12.25 a.m.	
	5/4/16		A light quiet on enemy's. Shelling seldom has been from ever day.	

4th NORTHUMBRIAN HOW. BDE. R.F.A.

WAR DIARY
or
INTELLIGENCE SUMMARY.
(Erase heading not required.)

Army Form C. 2118.

Place	Date	Hour	Summary of Events and Information	Remarks and references to Appendices
	6/7/15		A quiet day day on our front. Some Zeppelins 2nd Lot of refugees of which 1st Canadians had then Batteries went in by gap of which J Teche - STEENVOORDE	
	7/7/15		A quiet day. 2nd Lot of Simpl arrived. 7 Bdy completed 3.30. Col. & adjt Left for new position arrived down way as Group stafs arrived in 2nd Bde at 3-30 Col. in new position. Col. & Adjt went round from 1st Bdy N14, c9 & B
	8/7/15		7 Batteries & H Q arrived at new position 2nd Bde N26, c 9 S - TSC 2,6 Col. Adjt went round various times. 2" of 7 Batteries 3rd Bdy N21, a2 ais came in with anything
	9/7/15		Batteries wrote to various Battalions as battery T.C. a battery All our Batteries Watched daily T.C. a battery	
	10/7/15		Enemy again today killed much to what we sent up a wolf Heavy Battalion	
	11/7/15		Enemy shelling of every gun at our Battalion whom find used (Enemy ventilated 2 3rd CFA Bdy howly shelled. By shafs N of YPRES	

WAR DIARY
or
INTELLIGENCE SUMMARY

Army Form C. 2118.

4th NORTHUMBRIAN HOW. BDE. R.F.A.

Place	Date	Hour	Summary of Events and Information	Remarks and references to Appendices
	12/7/16		A wet windy with day. Considerable shelling by enemy	
			Of our front line & supports with heavy infantry casualties. Our heavy retaliation available and considerable destruction of our 4.5" & 15 Pdr Amn. A most unsatisfactory state of affairs	
	13/7/16		A windy hot dry day. Quiet on the whole	
			4 Battery ammunition. Our new emplacement	
	14/7/16		A wet morning. Our Old light Rohn battery carried knocks a attempts of 5.9" Johs. We retaliated putting one shell one for every 3" 5.9. Had immediate stop by infantry	
	15/7/16		3 Batteries in action. Very Quiet on western sector.	
	16/7/16		4 Batteries firing on 25 pdrs with 2. Cumbries & ammo filled	
			Casualties to 4 Howm P. & L.Bty W. att of 5.8 Bathy were wounded	
	27/7/16		3 Batteries in action. Very quiet on our front on 25 & 29	
	30/7/16		with rain. Round 3rd Div. & 7th attle Gulen fg. Our G.L. was killed. I 3rd D.V. The detachment of the forward Gun of 5th Battery of Mongersum was heavily gazed for 2½ hours during	

WOOLVERGHUM was heavily gassed for 2½ hours during very effective – Box respirator proved O.K.

Robert Chapman
Major R Bt
4th NORTHUMBRIAN HOW. BDE. R.F.A.

Lt. Hawkinson (Hon) R.A. RFA 777

2.5.3 Bde R FA

50

Vol XI

WAR DIARY
or
INTELLIGENCE SUMMARY.
(Erase heading not required.)

Army Form C. 2118.

Instructions regarding War Diaries and Intelligence
Summaries are contained in F. S. Regs., Part II.
and the Staff Manual respectively. Title pages
will be prepared in manuscript.

Place	Date	Hour	Summary of Events and Information	Remarks and references to Appendices
	1/6/16		Bright word to 1st Corps sound School Stenwerde	
	2/6/16		Sibley leaves	
	7/7/16			
	8/8/16		Wire received from 2nd Army congratulating 50'DA y this bde and by on 1st Division and Corps displayed in withing to the attack on 3rd & 24th Divisions (3rd & 3rd Division being covered by 50'DA) & the attack	
			On 11th inst a tank exploded in our midst. He was informed that an ordnance workperson was to take place at once. The officer in the Bde went to select out the 3 hollows and Land on to each of the gun brigades in the Div. One division by be immediately took D.A.C. Col. Greely proceed from Corps on 11th inst and took over duties of C.R.A. (You Korman being on leave) On 12th inst 2nd Welch E/A 1/4 join R.F.C.	

Place	Date	Hour	Summary of Events and Information	Remarks and references to Appendices
	14/5/16		Battery horses exercised. Information received Col. Hoffman & Col. Anderson were to proceed to England as Battery Commanders. Lt. McLean was instructed to join the 54th Battery in action. Orders made as to staff of a Division, Officers who occupied as list of Harrowville. There were Major: Lt. Col. Sholly, Major Burnes, Capt. Andrews for Willis (D.A.C.) Bickman, Ennis (adjt) Dunne (N.S.), Patterson (A.O.), Duguid (S.W. Soff), Oxendien (D.A.C.), Liuts McLean, Rutherford, McMahon, Willis, Middle Robinson, Blood, Dixon, Burnet, McCollum, Inglis, Capt R. Robinson D.S.O. Leslie & Lt. Smith were on leave, also Lt. Robertson (D.A.C.) It was decided to Illiarft a return of the Men on 6/1/19? the date General (1915) the date of Col. Jannon & Col Digis's men from tody. A list of all Officers wh were Embarkin is attached. All were Capt.ff ...	

Vol 12

23rd Northumbrian Bde RFA

WAR DIARY
or
INTELLIGENCE SUMMARY.

Army Form C. 2118.

(Erase heading not required.)

Instructions regarding War Diaries and Intelligence Summaries are contained in F. S. Regs., Part II. and the Staff Manual respectively. Title pages will be prepared in manuscript.

Place	Date	Hour	Summary of Events and Information	Remarks and references to Appendices

Army Form C. 2118.

WAR DIARY
or
INTELLIGENCE SUMMARY.
(Erase heading not required.)

Instructions regarding War Diaries and Intelligence Summaries are contained in F.S. Regs., Part II. and the Staff Manual respectively. Title pages will be prepared in manuscript.

Place	Date	Hour	Summary of Events and Information	Remarks and references to Appendices

Army Form C. 2118.

253 (NORTHUMBRIAN) BDE RFA
WAR DIARY
— or —
INTELLIGENCE SUMMARY.

JULY 1916

VOL XVI

Vol X/3

50

Army Form C. 2118.

253 NORTHUMBRIAN BDE RFA
WAR DIARY
or
AUGUST INTELLIGENCE SUMMARY. VOLUME XVII

Vol 14

(Erase heading not required.)

Instructions regarding War Diaries and Intelligence Summaries are contained in F. S. Regs., Part II. and the Staff Manual respectively. Title pages will be prepared in manuscript.

Place	Date	Hour	Summary of Events and Information	Remarks and references to Appendices
	1/8/16		A Bty and 252 Bde B+R 251 Bde C and 250 Bde	
	2		Quiet day	
	3			
	4		Enemy aeroplane activity in evening	
	5		C.O. visited T Bat; A quiet day	
			all day. Enemy Trench Mortars shelled our Bivouac	
	6		A quiet day. C.O visited gun positions A Bty shelled only	
	7		One man + one horse killed. Two South wounded	
	8		No A Bty rumours - for our one our colonel B.C. et 6 pm & the shop	
	9			
	10			
	11			
	12			
	13			
	14			
15				
16				
17			Co. of the area	

Army Form C. 2118.

WAR DIARY
or
INTELLIGENCE SUMMARY.
(Erase heading not required.)

Instructions regarding War Diaries and Intelligence Summaries are contained in F. S. Regs., Part II. and the Staff Manual respectively. Title pages will be prepared in manuscript.

Place	Date	Hour	Summary of Events and Information	Remarks and references to Appendices
	18/5/16		Orders issued for 250 & 253 Btns but to go into action at present	
	19/5/16		O/C Offr indently informed necessary ground war Cobie C.R.A. pressed	
			tactical column for all batteries near Cobie. Lines at 9/5	
	20/5/16		toilette horses & harness under Sailing Corradino	
	21/5/16		O/C visited Marfa for Funny Schum Bos. found By positions	
	22/5/16			
	23/5/16		O/C visited Imtarfa, Floriana Fortunes, en afternoon Fort B.C. & Bourge	
	24/5/16		Colles harness under saddlery arrangements	
	25/5/16		Baltrie horses under column 9 9/c Btre, or weekly 9 own Bns	
			do	
	26/5/16		do	
	27/5/16		do	
	28/5/16			
	29/5/16		Gunners a little I instruction outdoor schem 6 ams out to so' to bellum &	
	30/5/16		a steady and def visual contact 3 trees from sd to Ballum in the oven-foy	
	31/5/16		Our horses & harness during night Other occurrence night.	

H. Houston
Cap? Adjt 22 Mountain) Brigade.

253rd. BRIGADE R. F. A.

50th. DIVISIONAL ARTILLERY

SEPTEMBER 1916.

Army Form C. 2118.

253rd (NORTHUMBRIAN) BRIGADE R.F.A.

September 1916. WAR DIARY VOLUME 18.

INTELLIGENCE SUMMARY.
(Erase heading not required.)

Vol 15

Instructions regarding War Diaries and Intelligence Summaries are contained in F. S. Regs., Part II. and the Staff Manual respectively. Title pages will be prepared in manuscript.

Place	Date	Hour	Summary of Events and Information	Remarks and references to Appendices

1/9/16 — O/C Bde & Adjt visited Battery positions. B.O's obs of CRA Battery. Adjt to 2nd column. A.C Group to turn over 2nd day's firing.

2/9/16 — A.C Battery visited Position — B battery carried out salvos with Watch.

3/9/16 — A Battery carried out salvos with Watch. Ghost Sends in wiring at HQ's. Coy not moving. C. Bty below Front. 6 in Water. D/O 2/L RA in charge of position.

4/9/16 — O/C Bde & Adjt at 2.30 EBM — Brigade Conf — am 1.10pm — Battery Runners under Bdly Sergeant Cunningham took on 111 Bdy engagement. 27th Div arrived & ours Bde Group arrived - O/C Bde & Adjt at 10 — 8 L.G. Battery departures 1 Sub Section - D Bty joined up in Bly.

5/9/16 — O/C B remained strength of Bdes — 60m with 15 Offrs and Continued 4th about 7.30 — Bde Commander's Escorts took mess

6/9/16 — 1st Day of month all as ordered

7/9/16 — Last day Georgstuck — 1st Battery to turn — Conti large 1st Firing of troops & turn forward O/C Bty at his position

11/9/16 — Post Bde moved to Major Bura F.E OBE.

Army Form C. 2118

WAR DIARY
or
INTELLIGENCE SUMMARY
(Erase heading not required.)

Place	Date	Hour	Summary of Events and Information	Remarks and references to Appendices
	Sept. 15th		Attack on Divisional zone commenced at 5.20 a.m. Full particulars in attached notes. Hqrs Staff signallers kept up communications splendidly under heavy fire at times. The Brigade in early afternoon was suddenly ordered to move forward following the infantry advance. This was quite unexpected, as 251st Brigade R.F.A. had been held in readiness to do so. Arrangements re choice of positions, communications etc had to be made hurriedly, but all batteries did well. On the early morning of the 16th, three of the batteries were ready to fire and later two howitzers were got on. All these on the old barrage.	

WAR DIARY
or
INTELLIGENCE SUMMARY
(Erase heading not required.)

Army Form C. 2118

Place	Date	Hour	Summary of Events and Information	Remarks and references to Appendices
	Sept 16th		Busy day. Consolidating and trying to locate trenches held by our own people and the enemy. As the situation was constantly changing, it necessitated a considerable amount of hard work on F.O.O's and Liaison Officers. All batteries had an extremely hard time, and also the drivers from through the large amount of ammunition used, and the distance to the Wagon lines. Sgt. Sharp's untimely death is deeply regretted. He was a painstaking No 1, with a splendid command, and did particularly good work building strong battery positions at KEMMEL, for the projected advance.	
	Sept 17th.		Two enemy attacks on the 150th Bde front, covered by this Brigade. Os.O. Batteries still looking for suitable O.P's, and getting information as to the trenches occupied by ourselves and the enemy. Barraging and destroying communication trenches all day and night. In the evening a definite attack was made to clear the enemy out of the trenches, and this continued more or less during the night. In the end we were informed that our barrage had been effective, and that we had taken all the trenches previously occupied by the enemy from MARTINPUICH to FRESCOENVT. Information received from wounded Artillery officer prisoner that the gas shell fired by our D/250 Battery the previous two nights into MARTINPUICH H had neutralised the fire of enemy's batteries, but that their gas masks had been quite satisfactory, and no fatal results had occurred to them.	

Army Form C. 2118

WAR DIARY
or
INTELLIGENCE SUMMARY
(Erase heading not required.)

Instructions regarding War Diaries and Intelligence Summaries are contained in F. S. Regs., Part II. and the Staff Manual respectively. Title Pages will be prepared in manuscript.

Place	Date	Hour	Summary of Events and Information	Remarks and references to Appendices
	18th Sept.		Full diary attached. A very wet day, hindering operations. Warning order for attack cancelled. Registration impossible. Enemy made inroads into our gains and bombing attacks on both sides.	
	19th Sept.		Very wet in morning. Clearer weather later. C.O. still unable to obtain permission from C.R.A to visit gun positions. Adjutant called on Brig-General, 150th Infantry Bde, and afterwards went round gun positions. Diary attached.	
	20th Sept.		Further bad weather; roads in a fearful state. Traffic held up for seven or eight hours. Ammunition supplies considerably delayed. Bombing attacks still continuing. Wagon lines moved. Diary attached.	
	21st Sept.		Fair day, but roads still wet and heavy. We began to regain ground and by midnight had made considerable headway. Roads beginning to dry up, and ammunition supplies etc getting more normal. D.A.O moved dump. Diary attached.	

Army Form C. 2118

WAR DIARY
or
INTELLIGENCE SUMMARY

(Erase heading not required.)

Instructions regarding War Diaries and Intelligence Summaries are contained in F.S. Regs., Part II. and the Staff Manual respectively. Title Pages will be prepared in manuscript.

Place	Date	Hour	Summary of Events and Information	Remarks and references to Appendices
	Sept	22nd	Great difficulty in keeping up communications; linemen out all day. Also difficulty in keeping guns in action. Arranged with R.A. Signals to lay two new lines Balloon wire out to planes. Position of our infantry still rather uncertain. S.O.S Barrage ordered in front of PRUE TRENCH Later reports from O.P. " No enemy can be seen between our front and EAUCOURT-L'ABBAYE.	
	Sept	23rd	Registering by balloon quite satisfactory. Ammunition ordered to be reduced to 400 rouns per 18-pdr and 300 rounds per How. Very lights absent on front at night. 'Roving' battery fired continuously at transport etc behind enemy lines.	
	Sept	24th	Large fire reported in enemy's line, caused by 'heavies' our Red rockets reported on our front, but they were found to be enemy lights, and not S.O.S. Signals. No 1278 - Cpl Broderick, W, A/255 Bty wounded. 3084 - Gnr Kelly. B/253 "	
	Sept	25th	149th Inf Bde relieved 150th Bde. Further considerable trouble with guns. Quiet day. Three minutes bombardment put up at 12.35 pm; balloon reported bursts to be perfect. Parties of the enemy were engaged by observation from O.P. at five or six times during the day. Three shoots reported caused casualties.	

Army Form C. 2118

WAR DIARY
or
INTELLIGENCE SUMMARY
(Erase heading not required.)

Instructions regarding War Diaries and Intelligence Summaries are contained in F.S. Regs., Part II. and the Staff Manual respectively. Title Pages will be prepared in manuscript.

Place	Date	Hour	Summary of Events and Information	Remarks and references to Appendices
	Sept 25th		An enemy aeroplane flew over the batteries about midnight.	
			No 1216 Sgt Smith, J.A. A/253 Bty Wounded	
			3085 Gnr Wilson J.E. do "	
			631 Cpl Webb A. C/253 Bty "	
			3000 Gnr Johnston S. do "	
			2739 Gnr Christiser J do "	
	Sept 26th		Still registering by balloon.	
			Hostile guns spotted from O.P.	
			Wire received that COMBLES had been taken.	
			O.C. reported to C.R.A. his visit to positions.	
			Instructions given to A/253 and B/250 Batteries to move forward, at dawn tomorrow to new positions in HIGH WOOD.	
			Again considerable trouble with communications.	
			Continual barrage continuly.	
			No 2141. Gnr Cole, C. C/253 Bty wounded.	
	Sept 27th		A/253 and B/250 Batteries moved forward.	
			Rumoured that cavalry had got through between MORVAL towards BAPAUME EAUCOURT-L'ABBAYE, but no confirmation.	
			At 12.35 pm our Infantry reported in EAUCOURT "L'ABBAYE. Dense volumes of smoke coming back again.	
	Sept 28th		O.C. and Bde Major inspected new positions between MARTINPUICH and EAUCOURT L'ABBAYE.	
			C/253 Bty instructed to relieve B/250 Bty at forward position: this move was completed by 12 noon.	

Army Form C. 2118

WAR DIARY
or
INTELLIGENCE SUMMARY

(*Erase heading not required.*)

Instructions regarding War Diaries and Intelligence Summaries are contained in F. S. Regs., Part II. and the Staff Manual respectively. Title Pages will be prepared in manuscript.

Place	Date	Hour	Summary of Events and Information	Remarks and references to Appendices
	Sept.	28th	Batteries instructed to bombard FLERS Line, this barrage being lifted later. 3rd Corps wired for full report on wire on FLERS Line, which C.O. was able to give after his mornings visit, to within 500 yards of same. Short shooting reported, but none of our batteries firing. Infantry sapping up towards FLERS line: barrage lifted clear. Orders for reliefs on 29th received.	

1875 Wt. W593/826 1,000,000 4/15 J.B.C. & A. A.D.S.S./Forms/C. 2118.

Army Form C. 2118

WAR DIARY
or
INTELLIGENCE SUMMARY

(Erase heading not required.)

Instructions regarding War Diaries and Intelligence Summaries are contained in F. S. Regs., Part II. and the Staff Manual respectively. Title Pages will be prepared in manuscript.

Place	Date	Hour	Summary of Events and Information	Remarks and references to Appendices
	Sept. 29.		Attack made on FLERS LINE on Divisional front. Brigade made a report on condition of wire. Infantry got into FLERS LINE, but not being supported on the right, had to come out again. Motor transport reported by Roving battery at M.3.a.2.2. A report through Liaison officer, enemy infantry massing at M.22.a.2.1 O.C. 253 ordered to take up new position west of HIGH WOOD; these positions partially prepared by B/251. B/250 changed over guns with 30 Battery, 1st Division. Owing to late relief B/250 fired during the night, and handed over to 1st Division at daylight. Lieut E. Darling and two O.R. wounded in getting guns into MARTINPUICH during the night.	
	Sept. 30.		Liaison officer reports statement of prisoner that enemy had moved his main line three miles back. Information that Canadians were holding M. 14, and are lining up with M. 21.a. D/250 Bty got one section into action in new position, and kept the other section in rear position until known preliminary bombardment completed. O.R.A. reported short shooting; charge as far as this Bde is concerned satisfactorily disposed of. Heavy shelling reported by O.P at MARTINPUICH. Continual bursts of fire during night on roads, communication trenches and other points behind S.O.S. line. Programme for bombardment and barrages received and handed to B.Cs. New Brigade zone and objectives arranged with C.R.A. Wire cutting well done in Brigade zone, and enemy front line trenches well registered. Forward section of D/250 well registered. Sgt Stobart C/253 wounded by shrapnel.	

B Stevens

Lieut Col RA
Cg N°3 (Northumbrian) Bde RFA

253 Bde RFA
Vol 16

WAR DIARY
or
INTELLIGENCE SUMMARY.

Army Form C. 2118.

253 (NORTHUMBERIAN heading BRIGADE) R.F.A.   Vol. XIX.

October 1916.

Place	Date	Hour	Summary of Events and Information	Remarks and references to Appendices
	Oct. 1st		50th Division, with 23rd Division on left and 47th Division on the right, made an attack on EAUCOURT L'ABBAYE etc. 50th Division soon obtained their objective, with slight loss and got in touch with the Division on the left, but were later hung up and had their right left in the air, owing to lack of contact with the 47th Division. After trying to consolidate some of the positions on the right, they had eventually to fall back, but always held the old German front and support trenches. All our batteries took part, and later a communication was received from G.O.C. IIIrd Corps that the Barrages had been very well done both for time and height, and same was communicated to Batteries.	
	Oct. 2nd		Continual liaison between behind captured trenches are partly on the roads and paths. Weather very wet and roads bad. Later in the day Division on the right made further ground.	
	Oct. 3rd		50th Divisional Infantry relieved in early morning, by 23rd Divn. after having consolidated their gains. Artillery still remains in, and at 6 p.m. same passed from O.R.A 50th to O.R.A. 23rd Division. Instructions given for alteration in system of Liaison with Infantry and other two additional wires to be laid back for that Battalion, one to Infantry Brigade H.Qrs., the other at S.O.S line to the Artillery Brigade. Another wet day, with considerable communication difficulties.	
	Oct. 4th		Another very wet day.	

Army Form C. 2118.

WAR DIARY
or
INTELLIGENCE SUMMARY.
(Erase heading not required.)

Instructions regarding War Diaries and Intelligence Summaries are contained in F. S. Regs., Part II. and the Staff Manual respectively. Title pages will be prepared in manuscript.

Place	Date	Hour	Summary of Events and Information	Remarks and references to Appendices
	Oct 4th		O.O. at MARTINPUIG II and gun positions. Leave obtained from O.R.A 23rd Division to move further forward on account of communications. Adjutant inspected new head quarters, S,13,b an dparty was at once put on to clear up and prepare. Usual daily barrage as per O.P.A's orders.	
	Oct 5th		Quiet day. Brigade Headquarters moved to new Hqrs at S,13,b, arriving very late owing to traffic block causing delay to vehicles. Communication established and HW. exchange done away with.	
	Oct 6th		Generally fine, quiet day on the whole. Heavy shelling of front trenches and attack at night on the TANGLE. which was only partially successful. Instructions sent for next days barrages.	
	Oct 7th		Very fine morning. Arrangements made for offensive in early afternoon. Laying new lines alternate route to J/253. Communications good. Commencing at 1.45.p.m. an attack was made by IIIrd Corps on 1st SWB and right and left of same. The 23rd Division gained their objective, as did the Division on the left, but Division on right was held up and at dusk contact had not been obtained with them. The fighting continued during the night and heavy enfilade fire caused 23rd right to fall back to sunken road. Communications got bad owing to shell fire during very wet night, and as dawn Infantry Bdes were out off from front line. sassx seen Our O.Ps were busy with success, but Right Division were held up easier than our progress owing to smoke in the valley.	

T2134. Wt. W708—776. 50C000. 4/15. Sir J. C. & S.

WAR DIARY
or
INTELLIGENCE SUMMARY.

(Erase heading not required.)

Army Form C. 2118.

Place	Date	Hour	Summary of Events and Information	Remarks and references to Appendices
	Oct. 8th		A wet morning. After the taking of LE SARS we kept up a continual barrage day and night; one of the largest ammunition expenditure days lately. Brigade fired some 5000 rounds There was very heavy shelling on front and communication trenches, and our wires were out to pieces forward to forward Left Inf Battalion. A new line laid, this was also out. Bad light and few surprise targets. One man wounded at M.M.	
	Oct. 9th		A fine morning: light only fair, but improved later and we were able to cease barrage and observe for any supports or transport in front of Infantry. No movement noticed near BUTTE DE WARLENCOURT. C.R.A. and (Col Moss-Blundell) and BM called to discuss future positions for a further advance. O. C. at MARTINPUICH and gn positions. Great trouble with Infantry communications. Another line laid but cut almost at once. 2/Lieut G. H Wilson C/253 Bty to hospital. Shooting as per programme: roving battery, owing to bad light had few targets.	
	Oct 10th		A bright clear day with good observing light. New programme commenced and roving battery engaged with success many other targets various other movements of enemy reported and noted for future. On the whole a quiet day as far as hostile shelling concerned. Capt Cawston sent to C/253 Bty.	

Army Form C. 2118.

WAR DIARY
or
INTELLIGENCE SUMMARY.
(Erase heading not required.)

Instructions regarding War Diaries and Intelligence Summaries are contained in F. S. Regs., Part II. and the Staff Manual respectively. Title pages will be prepared in manuscript.

Place	Date	Hour	Summary of Events and Information	Remarks and references to Appendices
	Oct 10th		Bg. Genl. MacNaughton called at H.Q.S	
	Oct 11th		Bright morning; misty later. O.C. at conference of Brigade Commanders. New orders for Chinese bombardment received. Batteries continued wire cutting on GALLWITZ trench, and registering on the right, preparatory to attack in a day or two. In the afternoon, C.O. went with Capt Hilorns, looking for new gun positions; afterwards a report rendered to C.R.A 15th Div re positions. Night firing all night on barrage.	
	Oct 12th		Batteries registering and barraging all morning. In early afternoon attack launched. All our batteries assisting, the Division on our right. The attack was not a success, and with the exception of right, where line was advanced 50 yards, it was a case of "as you were".	
	Oct 13th		After the unsuccessful attack of yesterday, there was little artillery fire on either side; we kept up a continual barrage. The So. African Brigade attached to 9th Division, are now reported to have made some progress with posts towards BUTTE DE WARLENCOURT, but the situation generally was unchanged. 2/Lieut Witherington returned to duty.	

Army Form C. 2118.

WAR DIARY
or
INTELLIGENCE SUMMARY.
(Erase heading not required.)

Instructions regarding War Diaries and Intelligence Summaries are contained in F.S. Regs., Part II. and the Staff Manual respectively. Title pages will be prepared in manuscript.

Place	Date	Hour	Summary of Events and Information	Remarks and references to Appendices
	Oct 14th		A very quiet day, both on front line and behind. D/250 changed positions with C/104 and exchanged guns and sights. Night and day barrage on our zone.	
	Oct 15th		Another quiet day on our front. Night and day barrage. Nothing of note. O.R.A. 15th Division showed our mode of carrying ammunition on saddle to his Brigade Commanders. Lieut Hutchinson in balloon.	
	Oct 16th		A quiet day on the whole. Barrages as per programme day and night.	
	Oct 17th		D/252 Bty came under Brigade and D/250 went out to rest at Wagon lines. A wet day. Registering for strafe in early morning. Barrages and night firing as before.	
	Oct 18th		Damp morning, fine later. Ground very wet and heavy. In early morning this Brigade was switched over to right to assist 9th Division, in an attack on BUTTE-DE-WARLENCOURT. We fired from 5m 3.40 till 9 a.m. The attack was a partial success only. Machine gun fire held up attack.	

Army Form C. 2118

WAR DIARY
or
INTELLIGENCE SUMMARY
(Erase heading not required.)

Instructions regarding War Diaries and Intelligence Summaries are contained in F.S. Regs., Part II. and the Staff Manual respectively. Title Pages will be prepared in manuscript.

Place	Date	Hour	Summary of Events and Information	Remarks and references to Appendices
	Oct 19th		Weather very bad. Ordinary programme continued. No fleeting targets. Weather cleared about 4.30 pm and at same time Bosche opened a heavy barrage. Quiet night on the whole. O.O. at MARTINPUICH	
	Oct 20th		A fine clear day! Enemy fire on front less heavy than usual B/253 Bty pretty heavily shelled. Two gunners killed in the dug-out. Our fire as per B.M's programme. Bosche aeroplane brought down. At 5 p.m. heavy fire on front by both sides. O.O. called on O.O. 252 Bde.	
	Oct 21st		Quiet on the whole. B.M's programme continued. Further shelling round batteries and HIGH WOOD area. Adjutant at 50th O.R.A.	
	Oct 22nd		A clear day; misty in afternoon. Various straffes as per B.M. Various confusing enemy lights put up in the evening.	

1875 Wt. W593/826 1,000,000 4/15 J.B.C. & A. A.D.S.S./Forms/C.2118.

Army Form C. 2118

WAR DIARY
or
INTELLIGENCE SUMMARY
(Erase heading not required.)

Instructions regarding War Diaries and Intelligence Summaries are contained in F. S. Regs., Part II. and the Staff Manual respectively. Title Pages will be prepared in manuscript.

Place	Date	Hour	Summary of Events and Information	Remarks and references to Appendices
	Oct 23rd		Very misty morning: observation practically impossible. Very quiet day.	
	Oct 24th		A wet misty day; very quiet on the whole. 50th Divn Infantry relieved 9th Infantry. In laying wires to new O.P, Lieut Atkinson wounded. (D/252)	
	Oct 25th		A wet morning, finer later. Good deal of enemy shelling in LE SARS and EAUCOURT L'ABBAYE area. In the afternoon intense, and other batteries put on S.O.S. lines. Adjutant at Wagon lines; later arranged to move 'A' Bty to in front of 'C' Battery. Wire to new O.P in order. 50th D.A. pressed to get D.A.O to establish forward ammunition dump. Sergt W. Wallace, C/253 Bty, awarded D.C.M.	
	Oct 26th		Good light, early, wet and not so clear in the afternoon. Ordinary programme continued. In the afternoon, in addition to ordinary programme barrages, 18-pdrs joined in a short bombardment of area in east part of MARTINPUICH and Hows bombarded ditch in M, 10 s, for half an hour and a single gun position in M, 4, c, 5, 8, for five minutes. Batteries fired on an S.O.S. signal reported in M,17,c from 5.15pm to 5.30 pm.	
	Oct 27th		Showery with strong wind. Visibility fair. Ordinary programme continued.	

Army Form C. 2118

WAR DIARY
or
INTELLIGENCE SUMMARY
(Erase heading not required.)

Place	Date	Hour	Summary of Events and Information	Remarks and references to Appendices
	Oct. 27th. (cont'd.)		(H.E.) C/253 Battery gun burst by premature: no casualties. In the afternoon two batteries fired for quarter of an hour on S.O.S. call.	
	Oct. 28th.		Visibility good. Normal programme continued.	
	Oct. 29th.		Visibility poor, owing to mist and rain. Ordinary programme continued. Enemy Artillery very active against LE SARS and our front line in M 16 A. We retaliated.	
	Oct. 30th.		Visibility bad. Very heavy rain and high wind. Ordinary programme continued. 641 Corpl. R. Bright, Headquarters Staff, ⎫ 1005 Bdr. J.P. Matthews, " " ⎬ Awarded the Military Medal. 949 a/Bdr. W. Shadforth, " " ⎪ 4358 Gnr. T. Poole, D/252 Battery, ⎭	
	Oct. 31st.		Visibility good. Normal programme continued. Brigade Wagon Lines, including D/252 Battery attached, moved to X 27 O.	

F.Bowser. Lieut. Col.
Commanding 253rd. (Northumbrian) Bde. R.F.A.

Army Form C. 2118.

WAR DIARY
INTELLIGENCE SUMMARY

253 (Northumbrian) Bde. R.F.A.
VOL. XX. November 1916

(Erase heading not required.)

Place	Date	Hour	Summary of Events and Information	Remarks and references to Appendices
	Nov. 1st		Visibility bad throughout the day. Normal programmes continued. At 3-45 p.m. our batteries fired on S.O.S. for 20 minutes.	
	2nd		Visibility bad in the morning but improved in the afternoon. Ordinary programmes continued. Brigade joined in a concentration of JOUPART WOOD. Both our own and the afternoon enemy aeroplanes were active.	
	3rd		Visibility bad in the early morning, improving later. Ordinary programmes continued. Battery registration carried out on GALLWITZ TRENCH. A/253 temporarily attached to 71st Brigade. In the afternoon enemy air-craft were very active over our lines.	
	4th		Visibility poor in the morning, improving later. Normal programmes continued.	
	5th		Visibility good. 50th Division attack on the BUTTE: as a result many targets taken on by our batteries during the day.	
	6th		Dull morning, clearer later. Report that the BUTTE had been evacuated the previous evening and 151st Brigade had dropped back to original line. Fairly heavy shelling round batteries A.1, A.3, A.1 and B. Normal programmes. Both C.O.s took over from 151st C.R.A. and 253rd Brigade came under him. Waggon lines all moved to new positions near D.H.Q. area, difficulty in ammunition transport.	

Army Form C. 2118

WAR DIARY
INTELLIGENCE SUMMARY
(Erase heading not required.)

Place	Date	Hour	Summary of Events and Information	Remarks and references to Appendices
	Nov. 7th.		Weather again very bad: operations nil: a quiet day.	
	Nov. 8th.		Weather very bad; slight improvement in afternoon. Heavy rain again in the evening. Heavy shelling on our immediate right about 5 p.m. O.O. interviewed Corps Tramway O.O. re transport of ammunition as movement of vehicles impossible. Batteries instructed that all ammunition to be packed in baskets if necessary.	
	Nov. 9th.		A fine morning with rising barometer: very clear. Instructions given for B/253 Battery and a section of D/252 to pull out to Wagon Lines. B/253 and one section of D/252 pulled out successfully.	
	Nov. 10th.		Light good in the morning, falling in the afternoon. One section of C/253 Battery successfully withdrawn.	
	Nov. 11th.		Remaining section of C/253 and the whole of A/253 relieved by 103 Brigade guns being taken over. Relief complete 12 noon and Brigade out of action.	
	Nov. 13th.		Brigade moved to MOLLIENS=AU BOIS.	
	Nov. 16th.		At noon Brigade ceased to exist owing to re-organisation of 50th. D.A.	

Sgauyr Capt.
for OC 253 (Northumbrian) Bde RFA

www.ingramcontent.com/pod-product-compliance
Lightning Source LLC
Chambersburg PA
CBHW081435160426
43193CB00013B/2285